Aussie
OUTDOOR
COOKBOOK

Peter Russell-Clarke

Lothian
B O O K S

Thomas C. Lothian Pty Ltd
11 Munro Street, Port Melbourne, Victoria 3207

Copyright text and illustrations © Peter Russell-Clarke 1998
First published 1998

National Library of Australia
Cataloguing-in-Publication data:

Russell-Clarke, Peter
    Aussie outdoor cookbook
    Includes index.
    ISBN 0 85091 939 8.

    1. Cookery, Australian. 2. Outdoor cookery. I. Title.

641.5780994

Cover design by Peter Russell-Clarke
Cover photograph by Ben Wrigley
Text design by Paulene Meyer
Printed in Australia by Quill Graphics Pty Limited

FOREWORD

This a great cookbook! I love cooking, having been thrust into it at the age of thirteen when my mum went to hospital for two weeks. Dad, a hard worker of the old school, shunned the kitchen, and there were five of us kids to feed.

This little piece of history will give you some idea of why I love this cookbook. Not only does it provide enticing and genuinely workable recipes, but it is full of stories of the kind that remind me of my boyhood. It is 'Aussie' at its best.

Since Peter Russell-Clarke and I were boys, Australia has changed enormously, and for the better. Our eating habits have been transformed by people from across the globe. Peter has captured with his typical flair the best of these influences to create a new outdoor magic of Australian cuisine. Not only that, but you have Peter's illustrations as well!

Good on you Peter, and thank you for dedicating your efforts to Australian Red Cross, who will use the proceeds to help those unable to enjoy all the delights of this wonderful book.

Jim Carlton
Secretary General
Australian Red Cross

CONTENTS

4

INTRODUCTION

Aussie Outdoor Cookbook is written in the hope of raising funds for Red Cross and, if you have purchased it, not only I thank you, but all those people of goodwill throughout the world, who deplore the carnage of war, thank you also.

The officers of Red Cross spend quite some time organising outdoor barbecues. However, dear reader, the cooking events they orchestrate are often without enough food to fill the rumbling bellies of those who wait patiently for the simple food which will allow them to exist.

In Australia our barbecues are bedecked with sausages sandwiched between thick, red rumps of meat waiting to be sliced into steaks. Cream-fat-rimmed porterhouse rivals sizzling barbecue patties, which may be served with plump barbecued corn or roasted capsicum and potatoes. Sauces either sizzle in pots or wait patiently for a plate to pass their way. Salads, sporting all the green hues of a Constable painting, mix merrily with Van Gogh coloured accoutrements. Glistening wedges of watermelon as large as my Ghanian son-in-law's smile, beans and tomatoes, cucumbers and carrots, iced gazpacho and grapes gleaming on cheese boards — all are standard fare at the average Aussie barbecue.

Mind you, much of it may suffer from prolonged heat and the constant prodding and poking of the over-cautious yet zealous apron-clad male who is the aficionado of the outdoor kitchen. This gallant defender, who considers the barbecue to be an Australian icon, is more jealous of his marinade mixture than Colonel Sanders is of his herbs and spices.

What this book sets out to do is to list myriad recipes for not just the barbecue but for alfresco dining. The barbecue is only part of this outdoor eating exposé.

So, dear reader, dust off your sunhat and drape it with garlands of flowers and ribbons as colourful as a painter's palette.

The bold red cross

As a young school lad, my mates and I were indoctrinated with the daring deeds of the Crusaders — valiant knights togged out in chain mail, suits of tin and topped with helmets sprouting gay plumes plucked from fancy birds.

White linen sleeveless tunics, emblazoned with the bold red cross of St George, covered their breast and back armour. What heroic figures they cut! Huge broad swords clasped in mailed mitts, visors down, hiding any human emotion, solid, powerful war horses bedecked with finery, all combined to set a young boy's heart pounding with excitement.

The rights and the wrongs of the campaigns were not considered by we youngsters nor, it would seem, by the French or the English

kings. All they were concerned about was ridding their countries of the fearsome and troublesome soldiers who were left over from their all too frequent wars.

The soldiers were not paid between wars and so spent their time villainously banding together to rob churches and whole villages and towns. They plundered precious plates and tapestries, gold and other goodies, along with the odd maiden and/or noble who could be ransomed for a pretty penny.

Such marauding bands caused chaos in the kingdoms, and so the idea of the Crusades was accepted with acclaim. Bundle all the rogue bands together, ship 'em over to massacre and murder the Muslims, and capture Jerusalem for Christ's true followers. The Holy Land and heaven for the Christians.

And murder and pillage they did. The Crusades brought together the French and the British who, till then, had seen themselves as natural enemies. The Crusades united the Christians under the one banner.

Mind you, as soon as the Crusades were over, England and France were back at each other's throats again, but while there was plunder for the picking their combined forces ensured they vacuum-cleaned the desert completely.

Although the big, bold, red cross on the tunics of the Crusaders is the same as the international Red Cross symbol, it never entered my head as a young bloke that there could be an association. Of course not.

One was designed to herald battle and bloodshed, the other to alleviate suffering and pain.

HARDWARE YOU'LL NEED

As a boy brought up in the bush, cooking outdoors was called just that — cooking outdoors. The word 'barbecuing' hadn't climbed as high as the Snowy Mountains in Australia's food vocabulary.

We cooked on an open fire in the kitchen, or in a cast-iron oven which was wood fired. In clement weather, we cooked over an open fire in the backyard or wherever else we happened to be.

To make your own outdoor kitchen:

* clear leaves and branches from around an area
* pile flammable material together, start it going, and allow it to succumb into coals
* plonk a camp oven into the coals and rake them up the sides of the oven, and also scoop them on to its lid.

In my day, if you couldn't afford a little three-legged cast-iron oven, you would cut a kerosene tin in half and, with a bit of pushing and shoving, fit one half of the tin into its companion to form a lid, and there's your oven. Often the lid was awkward to remove and replace to check cooking.

If you don't need to bake or stew, food can be grilled over the coals. Toasting forks are mandatory in every outdoor kitchen. I remember some of ours were quite elaborate affairs which extended themselves by clever design means. Use your fork to hold chunks of bread to brown at the coal face, or sausages, chunks of meat, or cubes of vegetables, to soften and sear at the edge of the heat. A thin green branch of a gum tree will do the job. Sharpen it so as to easily pierce the food and then suspend it on a forked stick acting as a fulcrum, and push it over the heat.

We found corrugated iron was also invaluable. The wavy tin was simply dropped on to the dying embers or supported like a roof over the coals by four green branches or chunks of granite. The dips in the waves of the tin allowed the fat to run from the food, causing the fire to flare — much to the amusement of the youngsters. Sophisticated corrugated-iron users chose pieces of tin with nail holes which allowed the fat to drip uniformly on to the coals.

Another piece of equipment my family used was chicken wire folded over double. A Murray cod or glistening trout or two was laid on the wire, which was then doubled over the fish. A stick was threaded through the holes to fasten the unit, and another stick similarly laced into the opposite end. This created handles so that the netting could be turned after one side of the fish had blistered and browned.

An American, simply known as the Yank, introduced my mob to an ingenious American method of cooking which was used by the wagoneers who conquered the West. He called it 'plank cooking'. Where they got the planks from was never questioned by me or mine, we were content with the romantic visions of Buffalo Bill look-a-likes cooking buffalo steaks over roaring fires as they dodged the arrows of Indians who were no doubt attracted by the heavenly aromas.

The method is simple if you want to give it a go. Soak a large plank in water then place it over hot coals. The wood, of course, heats and gently cooks any food which needs a subtle heat rather than a fierce flame. Cook steaks or chops, which need more aggression from the heat, on the plank once its underside has charred and is turned to the sky. Throw the food on to the smouldering, smoking wood and it will cook efficiently. The smouldering wood chars the flesh and the smoke permeates the fibre in a most delicious fashion.

A bit of practice will make you perfect.

The purists of the ancient art of outdoor cooking would prefer clay. A duck, for instance, is simply coated in wet clay and then thrown into the fire. If the duck is not freshly caught, its stomach, and the tubes fore and aft from it, should be removed. Once the clay parcel has been in the fire for an hour or so, take it from the heat, crack it open with a lump of wood and release the bird. You will be pleased that the feathers will have remained with the clay and the flesh be moist and succulent because it has been efficiently steamed. If the plucking process has not been efficient, either pick out the offending quills with your fingers or simply skin the bird — a process I recommend, as you get rid of much of the fat.

A more sophisticated way of clay cooking is to pluck the duck or chicken, quail, sparrow or squab, remove its skin, rub it with oil and a little garlic salt, lay spinach leaves over the flesh, and then wrap the whole in a blanched lettuce or cabbage leaf. Some would now cover that in paperbark. I hesitate to recommend it as paperbark is not readily available at your corner store. Anyway, spread clay the thickness of your finger over the bundle and throw it into the fire. In an hour or so, take it out, crack off the clay, throw away the bark and/or outside leaves, and serve the bird with its spinach leaves dusted with cracked pepper and, as my family did, a large chunk of toast on which you've spooned clotted cream soured with wild lemon.

Without a doubt, I can say that meat, uncovered and unadorned, thrown into hot coals, then taken out, dusted down and eaten, is a marvellous taste adventure. Naturally, it takes a brave person to fling an eye fillet into the flames but, believe me, nothing will happen other than the outside will char and the inside remain deliciously pink, depending on how long you leave it there, of course.

Weber kettles, cast-iron pots, cut kerosene tins, chicken wire or corrugated iron are all still a bit fancy for a bloke I met up in the back blocks of Victoria's old goldmining area.

• • • • •

'M'mates pile a few stones around as a bit of a windbreak and to stop the fire spreading. All I do is cut a hole in the top of a hollow log with m'axe, put a thatchwork of green sticks across it, shove grass and twigs up the hollow log to get it going, throw on some bigger stuff and away she goes. You've got draft from both ends of the hollow log which sends the heat straight up the hole you've cut, just like it was a chimney. 'Course you've got to be careful to let the flames die down and the trick is not to get the fire so fierce y'log goes up too.

'If you've only got a small meal to cook, tip a small hollow log up on its end, stick a small stone under one edge of it to allow the air in to form a draft, dried grass and bark will get 'er going, then a few bigger bits to make coals, then shove a few yonnies over the coals. They get red hot, the coals are fanned by the breeze coming through the wedge you've propped up. That keeps the coals going, the stones hot and the heat directed straight up to yer hunk of mutton or half a rabbit which y'hold over the hole on a pointy green stick.'

Now, dear reader, that's nothing new. The Aborigines have been cooking with coals and stones since they found fire after a lightning strike set an old river gum and a patch of native grass alight. Often a whole kangaroo would be thrown on the fire, fur and all. The fur would burn off and the skin of the kangaroo char. The cooked animal would be dragged from the fire, the skin peeled off using long pointed sticks in the way that we use barbecue spatulas today. The meat would be juicy and moist as the flavours had been contained by the skin.

The fun of outdoor cooking is in the experimenting, whether you're cooking a sausage, or something more exotic. And it is fun, isn't it? Sitting out in the bush or in your backyard with a bottle of red wine, some good mates, and some food cooking. Mind you, you don't necessarily need to barbecue in the bush, you can whip up a picnic in an instant, and perhaps just brew up a billy for tea.

Boil an old billy-o

Billy tea is, of course, famous and rightly so. The Aussie name for an old billy can came from *bouilli*, the French word for beef which was

pressed and tinned for tucker to feed the troops during World War I. The diggers played football with the beef, and used the *bouilli* tin as a cooking receptacle. They boiled tea, made soup out of whatever they could scrounge from the countryside, and brought the idea back with them to Australia.

Here's how to make billy tea:

- boil some water in the billy
- throw in half a handful of tea leaves and let them circulate in the water
- take the billy off the fire and wait for the leaves to float to the surface
- bang the side of the billy with a stick and the leaves will sink ... or most of them.

A billy can is highly versatile too. If you are near a mountain stream which you believe is unpolluted, use its water in the billy as the liquid for a thick soup or a wet stew.

If you are lucky enough to have caught a trout, a yellow belly, a redfin or fish from the sea, take the flesh from the bones and boil them up. If you have an onion or a carrot or something of the kind, throw it in with the bones. Crack a handful of grass seeds and throw those in as well. After half an hour take out the bones and skim the seeds off the top of the liquid, and then throw in the chopped-up fish flesh.

If you've been lucky enough to find some roots, lizards or snakes, or even eggs, use those as well. We often become worried about what will go with what — I don't. I worry that I won't have enough food to fill the bellies of the mates I'm with.

I've eaten seagull soup with black-lipped oysters and wattle seed, thickened with grated yam. Galah, tiger snake and bush turkey have also made a marvellous meal. As does possum, skinned, filleted and chopped into a fine mince, browned in its own fat and then boiled in fresh water with a touch of vinegar, a chopped onion and roasted ground bunya nut. Quantities? Whatever God's favoured you with.

Our First
BARBIE
ON THE BEACH

Fishy feasts

Ancient Ally Oop and his caveman mates from the Dordogne region in France ate trout as they huddled around their fires wheeling and dealing over the cost of inventing the wheel. And, in fact, trout vertebrae which date back before the Palaeolithic era have been dug up in the Hebrides by clever archaeologists. So we've known for zillions of years that marine and river dwellers are utterly delectable!

Fish, including freshwater trout, formed an important part of the great feasts featured by the aristocracy of all nations throughout the centuries. One recorded banquet given in honour of Elizabeth of Austria when she entered Paris in 1571 had eighteen trout dishes on the menu. At one of the dinners given by the Prince Regent (later King George IV) at the Brighton Pavilion in 1817, plain cooked trout was served with a tomato and garlic sauce. There have been references like this one in 1635 which said: 'When we speak to one who is sound indeed, we say that he is as sound as a trout.' And of course there's the old English greeting, 'How's it going, old trout?' which is answered 'Swimmingly'. Will Shakespeare wrote about trout in *Twelfth Night*: 'Here comes the trout which must be caught

15

with tickling.' (One assumes he's talking about fish and not Anne Hathaway.)

Now that all happened a long time ago and far from Australia. After all, Will Shakespeare didn't live here and nor did the trout. Various members of the freshwater trout family were found throughout the Northern Hemisphere, but rainbow trout was first introduced into Britain, Canada and Northern America in the late

nineteenth century. Though even before then it was realised that the eating quality of trout is affected by the water in which it is reared. One writer, a bloke by the name of Hale, wrote in 1677: 'River fish as trout will alter their figure, some for the better and some for the worse, by being put into ponds.' Of course, in those days people did not have the benefit of farmed trout. Nowadays, shoppers can be sure of the quality of the trout on sale, or most of them anyway, because the majority of the commercial farms in Australia have fresh running water in which they breed and feed their fish. If you buy a fish which has a muddy flavour, complain bitterly to the cook, who will pass this on to the person who sold the trout, who in turn will stick it up the nostril of the trout farmer.

But if you are one of the joyous few who catch their own trout, make sure of the quality of the water in which you're catching the fish.

It's sinful to admit but our waterways are becoming suspect. I remember years ago I was camping beside a stream with a mate of mine from India.

'My golly golly gosh!' he gasped. 'We have not brought water to drink.'

'Poke your head in the creek,' I suggested, opening a bottle of chablis.

Why he'd wanted to drink water I couldn't imagine. Nor could I believe he'd missed seeing or hearing the water babbling past the tent flap.

'Is it clean?' he ejaculated, eyeballs rolling.

In those long past days I laughed, even when he explained that in most Asian countries the water was no more than an open sewer. We've got to step up the protection of streams. And step up our awareness that some aren't as good as they could be, or as they should be.

After that little commercial let me go on to say it is one of the reasons I'm not against the commercial farming of trout — which by the way aren't Aussie originals. The original eggs were imported from New Zealand. But then most Aussies have been imported from somewhere or other.

I hope you enjoy cooking your freshwater trout using these recipe ideas.

How to bone a trout before cooking

You can carry out the boning of a trout before cooking it, leaving the head and tail attached but with no other bones.

First, extend the stomach opening slightly. Then put the point of a pair of scissors through the stomach opening of the trout and snip the backbone just behind the head. Don't cut through to the skin. Now, snip the back end of the backbone, behind the tail.

With a small sharp knife, run the blade between the rib cage and the flesh until you come down to the backbone. Do this on both sides of the rib cage. Loosen the bones from the flesh with your fingers, then simply lift the complete skeleton out of the fish.

Now you can use the fillets, or stuff the fish and reshape it.

How to bone a trout after cooking

Cut along the length of the backbone and the stomach of the trout, removing a strip of flesh about 3 mm wide.

Gently lift top fillet's tail section and bones up and away from the bottom fillet. Hold the bottom fillet down with the flat blade of a knife.

Place the top fillet, skin side down, on a plate, then carefully lift off tail, bones and head in one operation. (If the head has remained on the bottom fillet, carefully separate it from the flesh and lift off.)

If you wish, you can then slide the flesh of the bottom fillet off the skin. Flip the top fillet over, and remove the skin.

You now have a boneless, skinless cooked trout.

STUFFED TROUT IN FOIL
Serve 1 fish per person

INGREDIENTS
1 trout
1 banana
aluminium foil
olive oil
freshly ground black pepper
pinch of dried rosemary

METHOD

- Clean and bone the trout leaving on the head and tail (see page 18).
- Peel the banana, leaving it whole, and pop it into the trout as stuffing.
- Take a piece of foil, brush it with olive oil, and lay the stuffed trout on it. Sprinkle the trout with freshly ground black pepper and rosemary. Brush the top with a little olive oil and then wrap it up, making a sealed package of the foil.
- Put the foil-wrapped fish on to a hotplate, and cook over a medium heat for 7–10 minutes, turning from time to time. The exact time of cooking will depend on the size of the trout.
- Open the foil packet to make sure the trout is cooked, then serve the trout (still in the foil).
- Cook one fish for each guest.

FLAMING TROUT

Serves 4

INGREDIENTS

4 trout
aluminium foil
2 cups beanshoots
½ bunch watercress, washed and chopped
1 red capsicum, sliced
1 cup sultana grapes
½ cup Grand Marnier

METHOD

- Clean and bone the trout (see page 18), and put each one on to a piece of foil brushed with olive oil. Spoon into each trout some beanshoots, watercress and capsicum, and then fold the foil so that it's completely sealed.

- Pop the packets on to a hotplate over a medium heat and cook for 7–10 minutes or until the trout are cooked, turning from time to time.

- Open up the foil packets, put the trout (still in the foil) on to a warmed serving platter and sprinkle with grapes.

- Heat the Grand Marnier slightly, set it alight, pour over the trout and serve straight away.

Whatta whoppa!

Before they built the Blowering Dam in New South Wales, Brandy Mary's Flat was a lovers' paradise. The youngies of Tumut would roar out to the willow-swept flat where the river gurgled and chuckled at the gymnastics of these locals in the back of their fathers' old farm utes.

More than hayseed was scattered to the wind, and wild promises were broken as rapidly as laughter raced up the hill to old Brandy Mary's house. She was an old spinster, who twice a week would totter down the steep eucalyptus-covered mountain to meet the mailman who was delivering another supply of firewater. It's said her tottering gait was due to her vast intake of brandy. Well, that's what they said, but actually the oldies knew her name was Bandy, not Brandy, and somehow Bandy was more appropriate to the area.

Y'see, in the old days the lovers rode their horses out to the flat, but in my day the kids fed their females brandy from flasks and one of my mates also fed the fish brandied worms. He'd marinate them in the spirit, then chuck the line in the water and tie it to the ute's light button. The idea was the fish would fly for the boozy worm, jerk the line, which would turn on the ute's light, and that would tell my mate he'd caught a trout.

One night, the flat was crowded with cavorting couples when my mate's light snapped on.

'What a whopper!' he shouted.

'How dare you!' his lady screamed, slapping him across the face with a fly. 'Get yourself some dainty little piece and see if she'll help you bale your bloody hay,' she bellowed, slamming the ute door, tripping over the trout line and then vanishing into the darkness towards Tumut.

Today all that's changed. Brandy Mary's Flat supports the wall of the mighty Blowering Dam. At its feet is a trout farm. No longer do lovers leap about. Instead, the trout are bred from fingerlings which grow into packages to be frozen and sold throughout the supermarkets over the nation.

But I remembered Brandy Mary's the other day.

I was at a trout farm when a young kid looking into one of the breeding tubs yelled out, 'Whatta whoppa ...'

Instinctively, I ducked a swipe, as m'mate did thirty years ago.

TUNA STEAKS WITH CAPERS
Serves 6

INGREDIENTS

6 tuna steaks, about 220 g (7 oz) each
salt
freshly ground black pepper
1 cup dry white wine
1 sprig fresh rosemary, finely chopped
6 garlic cloves, finely chopped
¼ cup extra virgin olive oil
2 tablespoons dry fine breadcrumbs
juice of 1 lemon
1 tablespoon capers, chopped

METHOD

- Put the tuna steaks into a bowl. Sprinkle with salt and freshly ground black pepper. Pour the wine over them, sprinkle with the rosemary and garlic and let them marinate for an hour, turning to coat the tuna evenly.

- Lift out the tuna, pat dry and keep the marinade, including the garlic and rosemary.

- Heat an iron saucepan on the barbecue grill, or use the barbecue hotplate. Spread it with some olive oil and cook the tuna over medium heat on both sides, basting from time to time with the marinade.

- When cooked, sprinkle with the breadcrumbs.

- Whisk the remaining oil with the lemon juice, capers and some salt and freshly ground black pepper.

- Put the tuna on to a serving plate, drizzle the sauce over it and serve.

FISH FILLETS
WITH MUSTARD AND PARSLEY SAUCE
Serves 6

INGREDIENTS

1 teaspoon salt
pinch of freshly ground black pepper
2 tablespoons olive oil
1 kg (2 lb) fish fillets, e.g. trevally, ling, blue-eye
2 tablespoons prepared mustard
60 g (2 oz) butter
¼ cup chopped parsley
¼ cup lemon juice
½ teaspoon salt

METHOD

- Mix together the teaspoon of salt, a little pepper and the olive oil. Rub this over the fish, then cook on the hotplate of the barbecue over medium coals for 4 minutes on each side, or until the fillets are well browned.

- Combine the mustard, butter, parsley, lemon juice and ½ teaspoon of salt. Spread half of this mixture over the fish.

- Put the fish back on the grill until it is sizzling, then serve with the rest of the sauce.

GRILLED FISH WITH HERBS
Serves 1 or more

INGREDIENTS

1 whole firm-fleshed fish per person, e.g. snapper, bream
olive oil
salt
freshly ground black pepper
fresh branches of fennel, or thyme, bay leaves or dill
mixed dried herbs
2 tablespoons brandy, warmed
lemon slices

METHOD

- Clean the fish, and make a few diagonal incisions in both sides.
- Brush with olive oil and sprinkle with salt and pepper. Lay a few branches of fennel across the fish on both sides. Put the fish into a hinged barbecue fish/meat holder. (If you don't like fennel you can use thyme, bay leaves or dill.)
- Grill the fish on both sides, sprinkling a few times with a little more oil.
- Arrange the cooked fish on a fireproof platter with a few heaps of the mixed dried herbs around it. Pour warmed brandy over, and light. Serve with lemon slices and Sauce Remoulade as soon as the flames die down.

SAUCE REMOULADE

INGREDIENTS

1 cup mayonnaise made with olive oil and tarragon vinegar (see p. 132)	2 chopped hard-boiled eggs
½ cup each: finely minced celery, white onion, green capsicum	2 teaspoons anchovy paste
	1 clove garlic, crushed
	1 tablespoon prepared mustard

METHOD

- Mix all ingredients together well, and serve alongside the cooked fish.

Barbecue ahoy!

Turquoise is a soft, restful colour, much admired by interior designers of distinction, arty ladies and God. Or he certainly did when he coloured the water off Broome.

I remember its turquoise colour, patterned with flicks of silver, dancing gaily to the magic of the gentle zephyrs and the brilliant sun. A rejuvenated pearling lugger snugly slid across the surface after leaving the jetty mid morning.

The chef worked industriously in the kitchen, the first mate stood at the wheel and the skipper chatted with his guests, of which I was one. A flow of chilled chablis ensured the conversation did the same.

'What fish will we eat for lunch?' I asked casually.

'Whatever the sous chef hauls in,' was the reply.

One of the fishing lines trawling behind the lugger snapped taut and then started an animated dance which resembled the figure-eight flight of a bumble bee. Within seconds a startlingly silver, bright-eyed fish was flapping in a basket on the kitchen bench.

I watched the dexterous movements of the chef as he scaled and gutted the fish. He removed the fillets which he sliced from the skin before cutting them into thin, bite-size offerings. They were splashed with lime juice and set on slices of juicy mango. This was our entrée.

No wasabi, no soy sauce, no ginger, or pepper or salt.

We ate with chopsticks, which are used by many people in Broome. The Japanese influence permeates the culture of Broome ensuring an exotic flavour to the lifestyle.

On the bumpkin of the boat was a device which held a barbecue that was swung out over the water once it was alight. Several whole fish were browning as their skins crisped. Lemon juice with garlic and honey had been brushed into the cavity of each fish, and garlic salt rubbed on the outside.

'It's essential,' said the chef, 'not to overcook the fish, nevertheless the skin must be crackly. We Greeks,' grinned the chef, 'have been doing it for thousands of years.'

Then he shucked some oysters, dipped them in Balsamic vinegar and stuffed them into the cavity of the cooked fish.

'I've taken out the whole bone structure,' the chef said as he carried the fish to our plates which were strewn with crumbled fetta cheese that had been soaked in oregano-flavoured oil.

'The oysters fill the fish out as well as give it an added texture and flavour ... and, of course, you cut straight through the fish without the bloomin' bones getting in the way.'

He also made miniature fish burgers, but that's another story.

GARFISH KEBABS
Serves 4

INGREDIENTS

1 kg (2 lb) garfish, cleaned and gutted with head and tail removed
2 white onions
2 red, green or yellow capsicums
4 rashers lean bacon
bay leaves
olive oil
salt
freshly ground black pepper

METHOD

- Cut the garfish into 3 cm (1¼") pieces.
- Quarter and separate the onions. Cut the capsicum and bacon into pieces.
- Thread the onion, capsicum, bacon, bay leaves and pieces of fish on to four skewers, and brush with olive oil.
- Sprinkle with salt and black pepper, and grill over charcoal until cooked.

Roy Bigfoot and the mud crabs

Mud crabs have been taking bites out of Australians for thousands of years, and for thousands of years Australians have been retaliating by biting back.

Australia's North has mangrove swamps — said by some to be the lungs of the sea. They not only help the oceans breathe, they also supply a home for all sorts of swimming, wriggling, crawling, sliding fish, with fins and scales, or armour-plated crustaceans with shells and nasty nippers. Snails and snakes, crocodiles and wading birds all share the muddy, twisty, root-entwined shoreline which is constantly washed by monster tides.

And the Australian Aborigine also enters this strange, eerie area. Through sucking mud, sometimes thigh high, women push their way to areas which they know harbour the mud crab.

Once the tide has run back to the ocean edge of the mangrove swamp, the women balance their way out on the roots, digging and poking with sharp sticks into the holes that hide the soup-plate-sized crabs. These critters have nippers which could cut a shovel handle in half.

As you may know, once the nippers fasten themselves on to an enemy, they hang on for grim death. Many a probing stick is quickly shortened before, with a quick jerk and flick, the crab is wrenched to the surface. With what I consider to be great bravery, the very angry crab is expertly grabbed behind its nippers which it frantically waves like antennae in frustration. With a twine made from woven grasses, the nippers are nullified, and the process is repeated and repeated in order to satisfy the demand for what is considered to be one of the great flavours foods of the world.

Many argue that the Queensland mud crab is a flavour unique to Australia and bettered nowhere in the world. Our environment is pristine, they argue. Our mangrove swamps are as they were when time began.

My mate Roy Bigfoot, the local Aboriginal king, and I had many a meal of the succulent white flesh. He and I would make up our beds on the sand looking out over the Arafura Sea and wait for his wives to serve us with the delicacies which they had hooked so recently from the mud banks. Our beds, by the way, were simply a scoop in the sand which was still warm from the sun. And we would lie there and watch the sun slide down the side of the sky.

As the evening became colder, we simply pulled sand over our bodies and slept peacefully, our tummies warmed by the wonderful white flesh of the crab, and the mustard, which was mixed with cooked and mashed yams, made even more interesting by the native peppers and spices cooked with them.

The rest of Bigfoot's extended family slept further down the beach — I presume as a mark of respect to the old king. I must admit I never asked, but there were other indications that he was the boss. One being that he was the only chap allowed to drink alcohol which was brought to his top-of-Australia hang-out with great difficulty. And so it was with reverence that we drank two cans of beer (the beer was Carlton Draught in the white can — universally known in the Territory as 'whities').

'I drink 'em because I reckon the black fella and the white bloke can be happy together,' the big black man laughed.

As we sipped our beer, the mud crabs were pulled out of the coals of the fire and cracked open with a nulla nulla. The mustard (the yellow liquidy substance behind the eyes which most people usually discard) was scooped into a wooden bowl, mixed with flavourings and set in the sand between us.

The cracked shells were handed to us both so we could pluck out the hot white flesh. Because the crabs had been cooked in their shells the flesh was still moist. Its unadorned flavour was as Nature intended and one of the great culinary memories I cherish. Hearts of palm were unravelled and, like thin sticks of celery, were used to scoop up the piquant mustard, thickened with the fibre-filled mashed yam.

On one evening, we were given a plate of warmed water-lily root with cooked and crushed monkey nuts. Over that was a soup made from the crab shells and the remainder of the claws collected and boiled in a mixture of one-quarter seawater, three-quarters freshwater. Roughly chopped bush plums and ground bunya nut were thrown into the water as well. Two seagull eggs were separated and the yolks stirred in, then the whites beaten up and drizzled in, cooking and stringing throughout the soup.

I remember some years later dining at Paul Bocuse's restaurant in Lyons on his Lobster Bisque and, though it was delicious, it had none of the magic of Bigfoot's wives' crab soup.

If you wish to make this soup yourself and you don't have access to seawater, or if you live in the south where the water is bound to be polluted, use fresh rainwater, sprinkle it with coarse sea salt, throw in the crab cases and, if you are not lucky enough to have a bunya nut, use crushed cashew nuts and plum tomatoes.

Crush some green peppercorns and include those, and boil the mixture for an hour. Discard the shells, stir in the separated yolks of two eggs and drizzle the beaten-up whites of eggs from the prongs of a fork. This will quickly cook and string throughout the soup. (To ensure the yolks don't cook separately, instead of thickening the soup, take a teaspoon or two of the soup and stir it into the yolks; gradually add a little more, constantly stirring, then slowly stir the egg mixture into the soup.)

PRAWNS COOKED IN THE SHELL
Serves 1 or more

INGREDIENTS

salt
green (raw) prawns, 4 or 5 per person
olive oil

METHOD

- Rub salt well into the shell of each prawn so that it is completely covered.

- Drop the prawn into very hot oil about 3 cm (1¼″) deep. A minute later when it has turned pink, which means it's cooked, pull it out, briefly touch it on to some paper towel to rid it of any excess oil, and then eat it, shell and all.

A bit of a raw prawn?

The ABC wanted a programme on prawns, so dutifully I drove to the top of the Spencer Gulf in South Australia and, with my television crew, bounded aboard a prawn trawler and headed off into the sunset.

The person who'd organised the adventure had spoken to the skipper of the trawler days beforehand to determine if there were adequate bunks for the crew.

'Of course there is. And tucker too,' the skipper assured.

What hadn't been underlined was that the request concerned the camera crew, not the crew of the trawler.

'We'll be pulling in prawns early in the morning, so if you and your mob want to get some shut-eye I'd do it now.'

He meant we should sleep on the couches in the area which was used by his crew to relax between shifts. My crew thought he meant take over the beds which were in the four rooms running off the recreational area. My boys promptly dived under the doonas and were fast asleep by the time the fishermen came below decks to drink their scalding hot coffee before they, too, grabbed some shut-eye. There was some commotion as they, too, tried to dive under the doonas which were covering my crew.

After a reasonable amount of confusion, the fishermen graciously left my boys where they were and slept on the couches and on the floor under the mess-room table.

That left me in a chair because all the available space, apart from where I was sitting, was occupied by horizontal, somnolent, fish-smelling fellows.

They were used to the violent rock and rolling of the little fishing vessel but my mob weren't. Suddenly the door of one of the cabins burst open and a camera assistant fell across a couple of sleeping fishermen on his way to the sink where he was violently ill.

'Get outside, ya dirty blighter!' roared the irate skipper as he propelled my bloke on to the heaving deck which was awash with very angry waves.

Another two doors burst open and equally ill TV types tumbled out and were instantly forced to join their companion who was trying to outdo the heaving deck.

As the bedrooms emptied, they were re-occupied by the ship's crew.

My blokes all had a metabolism that simply was not used to the violent action of the fishing trawler as it braved the unusually high and turbulent seas. Lying down did nothing to help matters, whereas I, being forced to sit upright, was unaffected. Also, as I was concentrating on writing scripts, my mind didn't dwell on my environment.

I found it interesting that the cameraman was not affected by sea-sickness either, probably because he, too, had been working all the

while — taking pick-up shots of all the paraphernalia aboard the boat, as well as the seagulls screeching and screaming around the swaying masts, or flashing over the waves, obviously directed by an inbuilt sonar which saved them from a constant ducking.

Once we reached the area inhabited by prawns, huge boards which acted as scoops were lowered over the sides, dragged along the bottom, and then hoisted aboard to dump their payload of prawns.

By now all the crew were out of bed, sorting the prawns from the other shelled and finned fish that came on the deck with the prawns. Seagulls set up a cacophony of excitement as the fish which were not acceptable were thrown back.

Most of the prawns were then cooked before being packed and frozen. The best of the prawns were frozen raw. The cooking method was straightforward — the prawns were simply thrown into large drums of boiling water set up on the decks near the sorting trays. I kept well away from them as they spewed boiling water with each buffeting of the still-angry waves.

The crustaceans were removed from the boiling water once they'd turned orange. They were then plunged into a bin of cold seawater to stop them over-cooking. The efficiency of the ship's crew contrasted dramatically with that of my crew who, although bravely attempting their tasks, looked like death warmed up.

The galley was well equipped, and I cooked a huge bowl of seafood soup which revived them enough to continue breathing.

Although I didn't have mussels or scallops on board, it's not a bad idea to include them if you can. Here's the recipe for that soup.

FISH SOUP
Serves 4–6

INGREDIENTS

2 medium onions, finely sliced
2 cloves garlic, crushed
1 tablespoon olive oil
3 medium potatoes, peeled and cubed
1 litre (1¾ pints) fish stock
500 g (1 lb) snapper or bream fillets, cut into 4 cm (1½") pieces
1 teaspoon lemon pepper
squeeze of lemon juice
1 tablespoon tomato paste
½ teaspoon paprika
pinch of salt
8 mussels, shells well scrubbed (optional)
16 prawns, shelled and de-veined (optional)
16 scallops (optional)
2 tablespoons finely chopped parsley
8–10 black olives, chopped

METHOD

- Sauté the onions and garlic in olive oil until the onion is slightly soft.
- Add the potato, fish stock, fish fillets, lemon pepper, lemon juice, tomato paste, paprika and salt. Simmer about 15 minutes or until cooked. (Don't overcook.)
- If you're using the mussels, prawns and scallops, now is the time to drop them into the soup.
- Serve as soon as the mussel shells open, sprinkling each serve with the parsley and olives.

FISH STOCK
Makes approx. 1½ litres (2½ pints)

INGREDIENTS

500 g (1 lb) fish heads and bones (snapper is good)
½ large onion, roughly chopped
1 bay leaf
½ large carrot, roughly chopped
¼ cup parsley sprigs
1 stick celery
salt
3 or 4 black peppercorns
2 litres (3½ pints) water

METHOD

- Place all the ingredients in a large saucepan and bring to the boil. Simmer for 45 minutes, then drain.
- Any stock you don't use you can freeze for another time.

Fish in the news

Fish is often in the news.
'Dolphins die in long line nets.'
'Fish contain Omega 3.'
'Another fishy deal in Parliament.'
'Fish oils lower risk of human heart attacks.'
'Jonah takes up residence in whale.' (Of course, we all understand a whale is a mammal, but it does have fins and it flops about in the ocean.)

This story is not about newspaper news, it's focused on cooking fish in newspapers ... but maybe that's news anyway.

I was brought up in Tumut, a town in the Snowy Mountains which, as any good trout fisherman knows, is where the biggest, best and liveliest trout play the angler a merry dance.

Before the Snowy Mountain Trout Farm existed, and other trout farms in the area, you either tickled trout (more on that later), used the conventional bent pin, or fashioned a springy sapling into a rod, whilst watching with envy the rich city people casting with Jarvis Walker or the like.

One day my mother's boyfriend, a timber cutter and a mountain of a man named Skinny, brought home a rainbow trout he'd caught in a creek up the track. He sat down at the kitchen table after placing the glistening trout reverently on the sink. He read the newspaper and drank a glass of beer. When he'd finished both, he soaked the newspaper in a sink full of water, wrapped the trout in the wet paper, then threw the sodden mass into the open fire.

'Skinny's lost his marbles,' I muttered to my brother.

'Lost his fish if you ask me,' he replied.

But we sat and watched events unfold which, twenty minutes later, Skinny did to the newspaper — took it out of the fire and unfolded it.

Miraculously, or so it seemed to me, the paper had not caught fire. I now realise, of course, that a thick wad of paper won't.

Skinny gently lifted the fish from its paper steamer, peeled the skin from the fish, prised fillets from the backbone, placed them on to a thin slice of brown bread and ate it, as he indicated to my brother and I to follow suit.

I remember it as being the most marvellous fish I have ever eaten.

On reflection I recall he didn't wash the fish so it still had its protective clear slime coating. He didn't gut the fish which I now realise is unnecessary as the fish was only taken from the water minutes before. The skinning process was obviously to discard any ink which may have come from the newspaper. The wet paper, naturally, kept the fish moist during cooking so that the flesh retained all its natural juices.

For fun, and in memory of Skinny, I often prepare trout the same way, except that I wrap it in blanched lettuce leaves before sealing it in the damp newspaper.

I remember my son, as a five-year-old, saying to a fish and chip shop chef, as he wrapped a piece of battered flake in newspaper, 'Why don't you cook it in newspaper, mate? My dad does.'

The Greek gave my boy a puzzled look, took his money, shrugged and went on to the next customer.

If I had my way, we Australians would be eating much more trout. With all that swimming it does, surely it must be healthy and therefore good for us — which, of course, it is. Its flesh is polyunsaturated and, as I remember, some nutritionists maintain it's either an aphrodisiac or helps our sex drive. I have no opinion on those claims but I do know that trout is terrific.

I often simply pan fry it in a little olive oil. The idea is not to overcook it otherwise the flesh dries out, therefore losing its subtle and unique taste.

Of course, trout and almonds are a treat, and have been in Europe and this country ever since I can remember. But once the Europeans get on to an idea they stick to it. Why not trout and cashews? Trout and peanuts? Brazil nuts? Or even walnuts? We should experiment with our food so that one basic thought can expand into one hundred ideas.

• • • • •

Now, before I finish, I must honour my earlier promise by talking about tickling trout.

I was taught this by my mate, Boydie Herlihy, an old bushman from Argalong, long since gone to the Great Trout Streams in the Sky. He would roll his trousers up above his knees, then walk through the thick grass of his paddocks so that the seeds from the grass would attach to the hairs on his legs. He would then walk into the water of the trout stream and stand perfectly still. Trout would magically appear and nibble at the seeds attached to the hair of his legs. Slowly he would ease his hand into the water, gently wagging his fingers as if they were giant worms. After an initial fright, the fish became curious and gathered around the fingers, which gently stroked their sides.

Now this may seem like a fairy story, but let me assure you it's true. The fish would end up curling around the fingers like a cat does around your legs. The fish not only curled around the fingers, but leaned heavily on them before the fingers, in a spasm of movement, flung the fish from the water.

I must admit every time I performed this trick I felt immensely sorry for the fish which, once I'd caught them, I'd keep in a miniature pond I'd made beside the stream.

My wife reminds me of the time I felt so sorry for them I actually let them all go and ate lamb chops that evening. But the next time I saw little lambs gambolling in the paddocks, I felt terribly sorry for them ...

Throw
ANOTHER BULL
ON THE BARBIE

I still call Australia home

Some little time ago I was in Las Vegas. Walking back to my hotel I was stopped by a cowboy who offered to sell me his watch.

'I've got one, mate,' I told him.

'You've got two wrists ain't yer?' he asked. 'I've got to win some money back so I can get my horse out of hock.'

'And if you don't win?' I queried.

'I've still got my shooting irons,' he smiled, tapping two holsters hanging low on his belt.

I hurriedly wished him luck and scampered.

I never found out if he meant he'd hock them, use them to hold someone up, or to shoot himself.

I was there on an assignment for a TV magazine and so had breakfast next morning at the Circus Circus casino with Peter Allen and his manager. We talked about 'Tenterfield Saddler' and 'Between the Moon and New York City' but mainly about his love of cooking.

'I cook beans in garlic like the Gods. Maybe that's why I walk on air when I'm on stage,' he laughed.

I asked about the difficulties of getting nutritious food in some of the digs which performers were forced to stay in on outback tours.

'It's a gamble all right,' he agreed. 'But I'd reckon the odds of winning are a lot better than playing these voracious monsters.' He indicated the gambling areas with a flick of his eyes.

'But not all meals on the road are awful,' Peter admitted. 'Though I have had my fair share of less than average.

'On one tour, I'd finished my performance in the local Mechanics Hall and headed back to the motel for a supper which the proprietors had promised would be fit for the King of England. I neglected to say it would be more appropriate to have it fit for the Queen of

LOOKS LIKE HE'S OVER COOKED THE STEAK AGAIN!

Australia. But since they were oblivious to who sat on what throne, I simply satisfied myself that they at least cared about food.

'We swept over the brow of a hill ready to turn into the motel driveway.

'The motel was a charred pile of smoking rubble. Apparently the kitchen had caught fire while my meal was being made. A pan of oil burst into flames sending the chef base over apex and taking the pan with him. All the things you would expect, happened, including the gas bottles exploding.

'Miraculously no one was hurt but most of the building was gutted.

'Undaunted the proprietor raked together some hot coals and threw a sheet of roofing iron over them. Then he threw on thick steaks from the freezer which, fortunately, was in a separate building to the main motel.

'The steaks were frozen when they festooned the iron; the outside browned quickly while the inside, being frozen solid, thawed slowly because the outside, being lightly charred, trapped the juices of the steak where they should be.

'We plucked oranges and lemons from surrounding trees and squeezed their juice over the steak. Fat and lemon juice drained from the corrugations on to another piece of iron on which the boys had spread sliced onion and potato that they'd dug from the vegetable patch at the back of where the kitchen once was.

'Usually I'd have objected and demanded extra virgin olive oil but, my dear friend, let me tell you they were the best onions and potatoes I've ever eaten. The zest of the lemon and orange was spread on top of the steak which was handed to me on a thick slice of toast.'

'Hang on, Peter, that sounds marvellous and a million miles away from a disaster unless you owned the motel, that is.'

'So far so good, I agree,' frowned the singer at the memory. 'Y'see they'd rescued a case of excellent Shiraz from the bar.'

'Sounds great!' I cried.

'And it was. It was the home-made wine we drank afterwards which severely wounded me for a day or two. One of the lads was of Mediterranean extraction and believed himself to be a wine-maker par excellence. Strangely enough, as we drank his offering, we readily agreed with his summation. It must have fermented in my gut, or turned sour when mixed with gastric juices.

'Anyway, whatever went wrong, went horribly wrong.

'One of the boys fell in the fire, another tried to shoot a neighbour's sheep so we could cook lamb chops. He missed the sheep and shot himself in the foot. The neighbour called the police, and I would have been arrested with the rest of them had I not been having a sleep in the fork of a weeping willow tree.

'My memory of the next morning is rather vague but the roadies got us out of town and on to our next gig.

'Whenever I feel like a laugh I get a large Texan steak, a lemon and an orange and a potato and an onion and a bottle of Shiraz. I belt out "I Still Call Australia Home" as I heat up my square of corrugated iron in my rather palatial kitchen.'

'No grappa, Peter?' I smiled.

'My word,' he replied. 'How else do you think I fuel my primus stove?'

BARBECUED T-BONE
Serves 1 or more

INGREDIENTS
garlic salt
1 large frozen T-bone steak (ensure the 'eye' is included)
an orange and a lemon, juice and zest
a potato and an onion, finely sliced
a bottle of Shiraz
a piece of corrugated iron to hold one steak per person

METHOD

- I use a sprinkle of garlic salt, though you may remember Peter Allen didn't. A spirit stove is optional but, as I presume we'll be cooking outdoors, unnecessary.

- Take the steaks from the freezer, rub fat over the corrugated iron, put the corrugated iron over the coals of a fire, and then throw the steak over the hot metal. Move the steak about so that you achieve a lattice work of brown marks on your steak.

- Squeeze orange and lemon juice on the steak and turn it over. Squeeze more juice on the browned side of the steak and a sprinkling of garlic salt.

- The fat from the steak will run down the corrugations and can be collected in a frying pan which you have nestled in the coals. Since most of the juice from the citrus will evaporate as soon as it hits the hot tin, squeeze a little in with the fat.

- Throw in the finely sliced onion and thin slices of potato. The onion will soften and brown, as will the potato.

- Once the steak has browned on both sides and is thawed and warmed inside, take it off the heat, surround it with potato and onion, and sprinkle it with the zest of orange and lemon.

- Hum a few bars of 'I Still Call Australia Home', and hop into it.

SKEWERED MINTED LAMB
Serves 4

MARINADE

INGREDIENTS

30 g (1 oz) mint leaves
1 teaspoon dried tarragon leaves
½ cup vinegar
¾ cup brown sugar
1 teaspoon dry mustard
½ teaspoon salt
½ cup butter
juice and grated peel of ½ lemon
½ cup white wine

METHOD

- Put all the ingredients except the wine into a saucepan and bring to a boil. Remove from the heat, cover the pan and let it stand for 30 minutes. Strain and add the white wine. Let it cool.

SKEWERS

INGREDIENTS

lean lamb: about 125 g (4 oz) per person cut into cubes
2 whole small green tomatoes per person
2 slices onion, cut 1 cm (½") thick per person
6 squares of bacon per person

METHOD

- Marinate the lamb for 30 minutes, then alternate the meat, tomatoes, onion and bacon on skewers. Barbecue, basting frequently with the marinade until done.

RIBS ON A SPIT
Serves 6–8

INGREDIENTS

1 cup chopped onion
¼ cup olive oil
1 cup tomato sauce
¼ cup brown sugar
¼ cup water
¼ cup lemon juice
¼ cup Worcestershire sauce
¼ teaspoon freshly ground black pepper
2 kg (4 lb) meaty spareribs;
sawed into 2 strips about 10 cm (4") wide

METHOD

- For the sauce, cook the onion in hot oil until it is tender but not brown. Add the tomato sauce, sugar, water, lemon juice, Worcestershire sauce and pepper. Simmer uncovered for 15 minutes or until it is thickened to your liking.

- Salt and pepper the ribs, then lace them, accordion style, on a spit, securing with holding forks. Push the fire towards the back of the barbecue and put a drip pan in front of the coals, under the ribs. Cook, slowly, for an hour until the meat is well cooked. During the last 30 minutes, brush the ribs frequently with the sauce.

Swaggie

My mother had lent me her 1928 Oldsmobile with wooden-spoked wheels, four cylinders, and canvas top — or I think it was, and if it wasn't, it was a Buick or a Dodge. Anyway, as a young man it was a grand conveyance.

I was travelling between Tarcutta and Tumut along a road reminiscent of a corrugated-iron roof. Recent rains had ribbed the road but, in compensation, greened the grass which pleased the wild, as well as the domestic life, no end.

A jolly jumbuck drank at a billabong, watched by a swagman under the shade of a coolabah tree. I saw him tuck something into his tucker bag as I pulled up, feeling slightly like the squatter mounted on his thoroughbred.

'Can I give you a lift, mate,' I called, feeling it should have been, 'Will you come a-waltzing Matilda with me?'

He threw his swag in the back, along with a black and white fox terrier dog which looked like it should have been staring down the trumpet of a phonogram.

'Got a jumbuck in your tuckerbag, sport?' I grinned as I double-declutched my way through the gears.

'Underground mutton, mate,' he grinned through his beard. 'But I sell it to the Yanks as chicken — they pay more for it, the silly buggers. I cook for 'em up at the hydro scheme y'see. They're finishing Tumut Ponds Tunnel and, once that's over, I'll be on the road again.'

'Getting a bit of practice in?' I asked as he eased his boots off his bare feet.

'Been over to see m'sister. She's a nun at Wagga, mate,' he answered. 'That's why I'm dressed up y'see.'

I didn't. His beard was long and grey and, though his hair was cut, I think it was done with a knife and fork. He wore a khaki army greatcoat and, although it was hot, it was fastened with those huge safety pins which the Scots wear in their kilt. I thought he should have worn a slouch hat, but he didn't. Instead, he was a-topped with an Army issue steel helmet.

'Must get hot, mate?' I asked, indicating the head gear.

'Bloody oath. And distributed evenly. I use it as a pot to stew m'rabbits in. Got the idea from the Romans I did. They used to use their helmets to cook up their tucker at the end of a day's march. Nothing like learning from history, mate,' he said, rolling a few strands of tobacco with crushed eucalyptus leaves in a Tally-ho paper.

I offered him a match which he refused.

'I never light 'em. The bloody euco would burn yer lungs out. So I suck 'em y'see. The eucalyptus freshens yer mouth and the Havelock Flake gives you a lift. Like putting a gum leaf in a billy of tea, mate.'

I nodded, concentrating on the corrugations.

'Not a bad idea,' he said. 'By the way, they call me Rabbit,' the swaggie offered as I pulled over to the side of the road. 'I hop about a bit, y'see. When they find out that the chicken is rabbit, I hop off to the next camp before they set the ferrets on me.'

I built a fire whilst he skinned the rabbits he had in his tuckerbag, then used the fat from around their kidneys to wipe over the inside of his steel helmet once he'd removed his socks.

'M'head needs protecting more than m'feet,' he grinned.

He then collected some grasses from which he rattled seeds into the helmet.

'They'll be a bit tough, won't they? Husks and all?' I asked.

'No more than cracked pepper-corns, mate,' was the answer.

The helmet went over the coals of the fire, then cut-up pieces of underground mutton that he'd rubbed with salt and flour were unceremoniously added.

Whilst that browned, along with the sliced onions he'd also thrown in, he instructed me on making the damper.

'But the rabbit'll be cooked before the damper,' I said.

'We're not making a bloody sandwich, cobber,' he snapped. 'Get on with it.'

I did.

When the rabbit was cooked we ate it using green twigs like chopsticks. He then dropped my damper mixture into the helmet and, whilst that browned, the billy boiled. He threw in a handful of tea, some gum leaves, and knocked the side of the billy with a twig.

'Saves yer swinging the billy, though I do it fer the tourists,' he grinned, pouring the brew into two enamel mugs.

He then produced a tin of maple syrup, poured it over the damper which he'd tapped from the cooking container.

'Cocky's Joy they call it,' he said, handing me a mug and a piece of damper. "Course if yer lucky yer can get some honey from a bush beehive, but this is near as bloody good,' he said, taking a bite and washing it down with scalding tea.

'It's hard being a professional cook,' he informed me. 'You've got to do yer own shoppin' — that means pushing the fox terrier here down the hole and catching the rabbits in a chaff bag as they come out the other end. Then you've gotta skin 'em and cook 'em before they go off, and decorate 'em with whatever you can. I often just chop up grass and tell 'em it's spinach. Yer can't tell the difference the way I do it,' he told me solemnly.

'And you always need onions. Y'see they don't need refrigeration and, though the outside might go off, the inside's always okay. Yeah, it's not easy being a professional,' he said, patting his dog and unrolling his blanket, laying it out beside the fire, lying on it, then pinning it to his greatcoat and rolling over until he became a giant sausage which instantly went to sleep, followed closely by his dog named 'Hair'.

I found out later the name Hair had nothing to do with the things with big ears which ended up being jugged but was associated with 'the hair of the dog that bit you' ... which apparently the dog did if his master got on the grog.

BARBECUED RABBIT
Serves 4

INGREDIENTS

1 cup olive oil
1 tablespoon celery seed
1 teaspoon paprika
½ teaspoon dried thyme
½ teaspoon each: salt and garlic salt
2 tablespoons lemon juice
1 rabbit, jointed

METHOD

- Mix together the oil, celery seed, paprika, thyme, salt, garlic salt and lemon juice. Pour over rabbit pieces and allow to marinate at least 1 hour.
- Slowly cook the meat over hot coals for about 30 minutes or until tender. Turn frequently, and baste often with remaining marinade.

How do you tell if it's cooked?

Many years ago, I was giving a lecture on food and cooking at the Town Hall in Ballarat, Victoria. I had just finished a most detailed and concise series of descriptive narrations on how the cook was able to most precisely determine whether the food, which had been prepared and then subjected to heat, was in fact cooked to the degree which would best enhance the flavour of the food, as well as ensure that it was visually appealing.

Satisfied that I had covered all aspects of the cooking process, I smiled triumphantly at the audience sitting glumly in their tiered, and somewhat uncomfortable, seats.

A young lad of ten or twelve, with freckles and acne, stood up hesitantly and then sang out in a shrill, piping voice, 'Yeah, but how do you really tell if it's cooked?'

Aghast, I listened to the audience applaud the little swine. He was right, of course. I had spoken at considerable length and said nothing. Like many lecturers I had assumed that the audience knew their subject and had really only come for a night out.

'Well,' I answered. 'If you get a fillet of beef and put it in the oven, close the door, examine the beef twenty minutes later to find it pink, you haven't turned the oven on. If it is black, you've had the oven on too high.'

'So have the heat somewhere in between,' piped up the kid, and then sat down, nudging his sister in the ribs.

'And examine the meat from time to time until it looks right. Then fearlessly cut into the steak where you would slice it later to proportion it for each serve. If it is cooked to your satisfaction, whip it out of the oven and accept the applause of your dinner companions.

'If you examine the meat and find it is too pink for your liking, pop it back for five minutes more. Remember that even though you take the meat away from the heat source, the meat itself has become its own heat source and continues to cook as you serve it.'

• • • • •

Prince Charles asked me, after I had cooked his Silver Jubilee Dinner, 'How do you get the steak to be cooked perfectly?'

'I put my eyeball inside the steak and have a look, sire,' I said.

I explained simply that, with his portion of meat, I sealed it on all sides in a pan of oil, garlic juice and a sprinkle of cumin and coriander in equal proportions.

'As each piece of meat has fibres of differing density,' I lectured, 'therefore the cooking time varies. So, with a sharp knife, I cut into the steak to determine how the cooking process is progressing.'

'But surely,' replied our future monarch, 'by cutting the steak during cooking, you would bleed the juices from it.'

'Simply seal it, sire. After all, you cut the steak to get it to the proportion you require before you start cooking, it's then sealed to trap the juices inside. So during cooking, if you cut the steak again, you simply re-seal it. The steak is turned, the cut pressed to the heat source and the cooking continues. But now the heat is able to penetrate to the inside of the meat, allowing the cooking to be more even.'

'Jolly good,' said Charlie, 'but on reflection I didn't notice the cut.'

'That is because I tucked a piece of bacon in it so it looked like a miniature elephant's ear. I then adorned that with a small nasturtium flower.'

'Well,' he said. 'That deserves a brandy,' which he promptly poured and passed to me.

I don't remember much more after that, but I hope you will remember that the basis for cooking most things is simply to warm them to an agreeable temperature for eating. Forget the rules we have been brought up with, such as, 'Beef is okay pink, but pork must be subjected to more heat for longer than a broiled Joan of Arc'.

'Why is this so?' Julius Sumner Miller used to ask. With pork it's because in Europe pork was susceptible to trichinosis, a worm which invaded the flesh and could only be rendered harmless by intense heat. Similarly with sheep meat in Australia. In decades gone by, few families could afford to eat lamb because when the lambs grew up they produced wool. When they became too old to efficiently do that, they ended up on the table as mutton stew or as a roast surrounded by a moat of gravy. Worms and other naughties, such as fluke in the liver, were subjected to heat from the wood-fired ovens or the gas from the early cooker range in the corner of every kitchen.

Australian pigs don't suffer from trichinosis and the majority of us can afford to eat lamb, which doesn't suffer from fluke or the like. So it is now trendy, and correct I might add, to eat our lamb pink. Pork should be eaten pink too, but most Australians are yet to be convinced.

I believe we should only cook food to change its texture or taste to suit our palate on the day. For instance, raw pumpkin is not one of my favourites, though I have served it sliced very thinly as its crisp texture and violent colour has helped the visual appeal of the food I was serving. But generally I prefer pumpkin to be soft. And to tell if it's cooked you simply poke it with a bamboo or metal skewer as you do a sponge cake.

To help cook a Brussels sprout you put a cross in the bottom of that cruciferous vegetable to allow the heat source to penetrate the thick butt of the stalk and therefore soften it so it is cooked at the same time as the leaves.

A potato can be placed in the oven with a skewer or a nine-inch nail poked through it. The heat invades the vegetable from the outside, whilst the nail transfers the heat to the centre of the vegetable, therefore speeding up the cooking process.

If you are cooking fruit, remember it doesn't need a helluva lot of heat. Feel it during the cooking process and you'll get an idea if it is softening. To really reassure yourself, poke it with a skewer. Of course, be advised by the approximate times which are usually detailed in most recipes, but never be too timid to cut it open and have a look.

'But,' you may say, 'I wish to serve a pear whole.' (By that I don't mean the vent of the pear, if they have one, I mean the pear in its entirety.)

Use the skewer, or if you are still unsure, slice it lengthways and decorate the two halves on to the plate with a sprig of mint or a dollop of sauce. Mostly this looks better than a rampant pear defiantly threatening the eater from its bowl.

Wild Pig Hill

Wild Pig Hill was an extremely steep, broad mud swathe down a high, pointed little hill in the midst of the towering Snowy Mountains.

I'd assumed it was named Wild Pig Hill because that's where the wild pigs rooted and snorted through the snow gums and tangled undergrowth. But it wasn't. It was named after Wild Pig Donovan who hunted the boar and the sow and the piglet and anything else he could lay his hands on.

It wasn't his madness with a firearm that had him so labelled. It was his driving.

To say Wild Pig had the manners of a pig is disparaging to the pig fraternity who, as far as I have discerned, behave in a proper and orderly manner until cornered by someone who wishes to shoot them and cut their throat, boil them, skin them, chop them up and hang them in a butcher's shop. Goodness gracious me, so would I be upset in the same position.

Wild Pig drove a porky size F100. It was even painted pork pink. He was a huge, porky-proportioned man with a flat, flaring red nose, bristly red hair and small, bright, red-rimmed eyes. Not even his red heeler seemed to like Wild Pig.

I'd only heard the dog addressed as 'Hey!' and whether that was because he constantly cowered in the back of the ute where inevitably there was a windrow of dirty hay, or whether it was short for 'Hey, you!' I'm uncertain.

The dog snapped and snarled at everyone except Wild Pig, and I'm sure he only desisted because he was frightened of contracting rabies.

Wild Pig drank rum, the money for which he made by selling haunches of hog, or what he called suckling pig, to some unscrupulous spit-roast operators. He also manufactured his own pork sausages.

His forays into the scrub were legendary. Most folk who go into pig country are extremely careful and timorous of the huge tusked pigs that inhabit the dark, tangled growth in their range. But it was said that it was the animals that were petrified of Wild Pig. He blasted away at anything that moved, or that Hey had cornered in a dead-end gully or the like.

Now and again a crafty tusker would get him, slashing his leg or arm as cleanly as a butcher butterflies a steak, but our anti-hero always won the battle. Or he did until a balmy spring day in September.

The Rambo ratbag had shot a sow dead and was about to kill off her three piglets when God intervened.

Wild Pig squinted down the scopes mounted on his rifle barrel at the confused eyeball of the young piglet. Before the killer's finger could press the trigger, a massive branch of an elderly gum crashed from the central trunk on to the noggin of the hunter, squashing him as flat as a night-soil carter's hat.

Wild Pig never moved of his own volition again. Neither the pigs or other wild animals disturbed the dead man. Nor did anybody look for him and it seemed nobody cared.

Of course, comment was made when Hey, the red heeler, appeared at the pub without his owner.

'It's the first time he's ever walked into the place,' commented the publican. 'Wild Pig always had him tied up in the back of the ute. He looks happy enough, though, doesn't he?'

The dog became a fixture in the pub, and Wild Pig was never mentioned again, except to explain the pig of a hill where a rusting ute was being claimed by the scrub.

It's said if you're passing the spot around midnight during the full moon, you can hear the wild pigs laughing, though some unromantic visitors say it's the frogs.

ROAST SUCKLING PIG

Serves 15–20

INGREDIENTS

1 suckling pig about 3 kg (6 lb)
pig's heart and liver
1 clove garlic
brandy
melted butter
1 cup water

1 tablespoon each: grated onion,
chopped parsley, green pepper
1½ tablespoons plain flour
extra 1½ tablespoons butter
1 red apple
watercress, baked apples
and cherries for garnish

METHOD

- Take a young suckling pig and wash it in cold water, changing the water 2 or 3 times. Rub dry, then rub inside with a cut clove of garlic and brush with brandy. Tie forelegs and hind legs separately and close under the body. Wipe the pig with a damp cloth and then with a lot of melted butter.

- Take a sharp pointed knife and make many little slashes all over the top of the pig so that fat can drip down into a roasting pan. Put a block of wood into the pig's mouth to keep it open for the apple which will be inserted later. Cover the ears, tail and eye sockets with foil to prevent them burning. Thread the pig on a spit and cook for 2 to 3 hours until the meat is tender and thoroughly cooked. Baste often with fat from the catching pan under the pig.

- While the pig is roasting, boil the heart in 1 cup of water to make sauce. When it's almost tender, add liver, onion, parsley and green pepper. Cook until are tender. Chop or blend the heart and liver, then mix with the catching pan gravy and some of the cooking liquid. Skim off fat and thicken the sauce with the flour kneaded with extra butter. Cook a few minutes and keep it hot.

- Pop roast pig on a large hot platter, replace block of wood with the apple, then rub skin of pig thoroughly with butter until it's shiny and crisp. Garnish with watercress and baked apples topped with cherries and put a cherry necklace on the pig.

- Serve with an apple sauce to which you've added an equal quantity of horseradish sauce.

Fun With
FOWL

Murder Most Foul!

The newspaper rustles in the sensitive fingers of Sherlock Holmes as he turns the pages of the *Times* to finish a story which had screamed its headlines on the front page.

Some foul deed had been perpetrated on an innocent and unsuspecting resident of London Town.

No doubt Watson and the great detective would solve the conundrum posed by the administration of poison or the application of a blunt instrument to a fragile skull.

It would seem that, without a Conan Doyle, such preposterous happenings are not recorded, in a literary sense, yet they are happening with even greater regularity than in those days when the super sleuths rattled around London's cobblestones in their hansom cabs.

Murders most foul are a constant part of many of our meals. Fowl of every form are mistreated by insensitive and callous chefs. Duck, chicken, pigeon, turkey and peacock are pummelled and bashed, boiled and barbecued, braised and sautéed, into something which resembles a product which could be successfully used as roof insulation.

We Australians have a history of throwing haunches of meat on to fierce fires to blacken and char the flesh. Little has changed except we now cut the meat into smaller portions. Mind you, we still murder it.

When was the last time you went to a barbecue and the male cook did anything other than drink grog and push meat about over fierce flames or fat-saturated hotplates until the proposed offerings had drastically reduced in size, become blacker than some of Tyson's moods and, when masticated, showed no hint of flavour whatsoever?

But now it's not only red meat which we treat as the Spanish treated a heretic. We cook pork as badly as I've heard some of our native cousins once cooked 'long pork'.

But it's the outdoor cooking of chicken I wish to dissect in this chapter.

The flesh of chicken or, for that matter, any fowl must be treated with compassion. Every skerrick of moisture must be maintained except, maybe, for the skin which can be crisped delightfully but, I must warn, not at the expense of the body of flesh.

A chicken breast, cut from the bone, the skin removed, and gently warmed in a pan licked with olive oil is lovely. A breast slurped with white wine and wrapped in foil is fabulous. The whole carcase, popped in an oven bag, is beautiful. But remember not to overcook. Chicken only needs to be warmed so that the grey-pink tinge is taken from the flesh.

We often hear today that chickens no longer taste like chickens, or duck, or any other fowl. But maybe its more because of the treatment we cooks have given it rather than the farmer.

Here is one of my favourite ways of cooking a chicken outdoors.

Outdoor Chicken
Serves 3–4

Ingredients

1 x 2 kg (4 lb) chicken
1 teaspoon salt
freshly ground black pepper
½ cup chopped celery leaves
¼ cup chopped parsley
¼ cup chopped onion
2 tablespoons olive oil

Method

- Wash the chicken and pat dry with paper towels.
- Rub the body cavity with salt and pepper. Mix together the celery leaves, parsley, onion and oil, and place in the body cavity. Fasten the neck skin to the back with a skewer. Tie with cord to hold the skewer.
- Place a holding fork on the rod of a barbecue spit, tines towards the point. Insert the rod through the chicken (press tines firmly into the breast meat).
- Using 60 cm (2') of cord, start at the back; loop around each wing tip (make slip knots so wings can't straighten). Tie in the centre, leaving equal ends. Next take a 45 cm (1½') piece of cord and loop it around the tail, then around the crossed legs. Tie very tightly to hold bird securely on the rod, leaving equal ends. Pull together the cords attached to wings and legs. Tie tightly. Adjust the holding forks and fasten screws tightly.
- Place the chicken on the rotisserie, with medium coals at the back and front of the chicken and a drip pan under the revolving bird.
- Roast the chicken for about 2 hours without the barbecue hood, or about 1¾ hours with the barbecue hood down.

BASTING SAUCE

INGREDIENTS

¼ cup tomato sauce
dash of Worcestershire sauce
2 tablespoons lemon juice
2 tablespoons olive oil
2 tablespoons Dijon mustard

METHOD

- Mix together the tomato sauce, Worcestershire sauce, lemon juice, olive oil and prepared mustard to make the basting sauce. Use to baste the chicken occasionally during the last 30 minutes of cooking.

ROAST DUCK AND POMEGRANATES IN A WALNUT SAUCE

Serves 6

INGREDIENTS

1 x 2–3 kg (4–6 lb) duckling (with giblets)
600 ml (20 fl oz) water
salt
freshly ground black pepper
1 small whole onion
fresh pomegranate, lime slices and walnuts, to garnish

SAUCE

INGREDIENTS

2 tablespoons olive oil
1 onion, finely chopped
175 g (5½ oz) ground walnuts
225 ml (7 fl oz) fresh pomegranate juice, hand squeezed
1 teaspoon sugar
3 tablespoons fresh lime juice

METHOD

• Put the giblets (except the liver) and the neck, into a small saucepan with the water. Bring it to the boil, then skim any scum from the surface, pop on a lid, and simmer gently for 45 minutes.

• Wipe the duckling inside and out, then season the cavity with salt and pepper and put the whole onion inside. Truss the bird, prick the skin, and rub all over with salt. Place it upside down in a roasting dish and pour in 3 tablespoons of water.

• Roast the duckling at 190°C (375°F) for 45 minutes, then turn it over and roast for a further 50 minutes. To check that it is cooked, insert a skewer into the thigh; if the juices are clear then it is cooked.

- Whilst the duckling is cooking, prepare the sauce. Heat the oil and fry the onion until it's golden, then take the pan from the heat and stir in the ground walnuts.

- Put the pan back on the heat and stir in the pomegranate juice, which should be hand squeezed so as not to include the bitter pith.

- Strain the giblet stock and add it to the sauce with the sugar and lime juice. Cover and simmer gently for 30 minutes or until the sauce has thickened.

- Take the duckling from the oven, pour off the fat and add the juices from the duck cavity to the pan juices, then add both to the sauce.

- Taste and adjust the seasoning. Simmer the sauce, stirring all the time for 3 minutes.

- Carve the duckling and serve with the sauce.

FOUR SEASONS CHICKEN
Serves 4

INGREDIENTS

1 x 1.5 kg (3 lb) chicken
freshly ground black pepper
good pinch of dried tarragon leaves
4 tablespoons butter
good pinch of dried marjoram leaves
good pinch of dried oregano leaves
good pinch of mustard seeds
soy sauce
juice of one lemon
vermouth

METHOD

- Dry the chicken inside and out with paper towel and sprinkle with freshly ground black pepper. Sprinkle the tarragon on a tablespoon of butter, gently lift the chicken skin above one side of the breast and stuff with butter and tarragon. Sprinkle the marjoram on another tablespoon of butter, lift the chicken skin on the other side of the breast and stuff that with the butter and marjoram. Pull the skin back into place to protect the delicate flesh of the breast.

- Make a slit in the skin over each drumstick, lift it, and stuff one drumstick with a tablespoon of butter with oregano sprinkled over it and the other drumstick with the rest of the butter and mustard seeds. In a large oven bag, put a dash of soy sauce, the lemon juice and a splash of vermouth. Pop the chicken into the bag, tie the bag and puncture it a few times near the tie, then put it into the oven in a baking dish and cook at 190°C (375°F) for 35 minutes. A barbecue with a hood is equally suitable for cooking this dish.

- Take it out of the bag, allow to cool, and serve.

Cooking chicken wings n' things

Chicken wings, popped on the barbecue, crisp and brown nicely with little effort necessary from the chef. Just as they start to brown, they can be drizzled with honey and sprinkled with sesame seeds, and then put back on the heat for the honey to warm and the sesame seeds to toast.

- Or simply sprinkle the wings with garlic salt and cracked pepper.
- Or splash them liberally with lemon juice.
- Or marinate them in soy sauce, honey and ground ginger before they go on the barbecue.
- Or, if you've forgotten to marinate them, once they've browned, splash them with soy sauce and a dribble of honey and finely chopped fresh ginger.
- Or, brush with olive oil, and, just before you serve them, sprinkle them with fresh or dried oregano, or basil, or both.

There is no argument in my mind that chicken wings are delicious. Simply barbecued and unadorned, or with the flavours I've suggested, or any others which may take your fancy.

A chicken breast, roughly cubed and thrown on to the barbecue and treated in the same fashion as the chicken wings, is also delicious. But a warning: DO NOT OVERCOOK THE CHICKEN BREAST PIECES. It is imperative they remain moist and succulent. Keep moving them over the hotplate which you've splashed with a good quality olive oil. The 2 cm ($1^3/_4''$) square cubes should take no more than a minute to cook. And remember, they will continue to cook once you remove them from the heat and place them on a plate with a crisp multi-green salad.

If you prefer the barbecue flame to lick your food, be extremely careful not to burn the chicken wings, as the fat from them will enrage the flame into fierce tongues.

The chicken breast, with the skin attached, needs the same caution. But, if you have removed the skin, you have eliminated the problem. Though if you have brushed the full breast with oil (one wouldn't cube the flesh to cook it over an open flame for the obvious reason it would drop between the barbecue bars), the oil will excite the flames, so keep turning the breast so it browns without burning. Add the flavours I've suggested for the chicken wings once you have removed the flesh from the flame.

And, by the way, the same principles apply to spare ribs or a slice of steak, a lamb chop or a slice of liver. Much of the fun of cooking is devising your own combination of flavours and visuals.

CHARCOALED TURKEY PIECES
Makes 10–12 pieces

INGREDIENTS

1 x 3.5 kg (7 lb) turkey
¼ cup olive oil
¼ cup soy sauce
1 tablespoon honey
1 teaspoon ground ginger
1 teaspoon dry mustard
1 clove garlic, crushed

METHOD

- Cut the turkey into pieces — wings, drumsticks, thighs, 4 breast pieces and 2 back pieces.

- Combine the remaining ingredients for marinade. Put the turkey pieces in the marinade, and leave for 2 hours at room temperature or overnight in the fridge.

- Put the drumsticks and thighs on the barbecue grill above medium hot coals and cook for 30 minutes, turning occasionally. Put the rest of the bird on the grill beside them and continue to cook a further 30 minutes, still turning. Baste with the marinade, and cook until clear juice escapes from a hole made by a skewer pushed into the drumstick.

PINEAPPLE CHICKEN
Serves 6

INGREDIENTS

1 tablespoon oil
6 large chicken breasts
1 teaspoon good-quality Indian curry powder
1 clove garlic, crushed
½ cup chicken stock
1 cup cultured sour cream
2 cups fresh, peeled, cored pineapple chunks
¼ cup chopped red capsicum

METHOD

- Heat the oil in a large heavy frying pan. Drop in the chicken breasts, and cook on both sides over medium heat until they turn white.

- Stir in the curry powder and garlic, then the chicken stock, and continue cooking until the chicken is just done. It'll only take a few minutes — don't overcook it, it should still be plump and moist.

- Lift out the chicken on to a warmed serving dish, and cover. Add the sour cream, pineapple pieces and capsicum to the pan. Stir to heat through. Pour over the chicken, and serve.

Vegie
BARBIE

A bloomin' rainbow

'Throw another capsicum on the barbie,' may not have been Paul Hogan's style and, those years back, when our Aussie larrikin flung prawns all over the place (for the American market they were shrimps) it was not considered manly. But thank goodness, dear reader, we've progressed since then.

Today, you are not labelled a namby-pamby if you enjoy the finest of foods and are of genteel manner. Vegetarians are no longer considered freaks with food fads they've got from some rocky outcrop in the Himalayas — handed to them by some goofy guru in a nightdress and with bad teeth.

No, today we're more enlightened. Or at least some of us are. Now vegetables on barbecues have become an absolute must.

I had a redneck mate of mine nearly explode with indignation when I invited him to a barbecue and served him a mixture of chopped fruit and vegetables which I'd quickly grilled on the barbecue.

'Where's the bloody chops and sausages, ya little pooftah? I don't mind a fair go, but this stuff will give you wind for a bloody week. It's bloody girls' food. It's like being served up a plate of mixed coloured confetti. Serve the bloody man meat is part of the Australian psyche and everybody but you knows it.'

Scowling at his plate of barbecued vegetables, he sulked off into a corner of the garden.

'You bloody beauty!' bellowed a voice from the other side of the camellia bush. 'It tastes terrific, mate!' roared the voice of m'mate as he swept back to the barbecue. 'Mind you I got some bacon cooked by the blokes next door so m'system didn't go into a state of complete shock. But the chargrilled tomatoes were terrific and you couldn't cop a sweeter taste than the corn on the cob with that butter and basil.

'I apologise about the confetti comment, cobber. It was just all those bright colours confused me for a bit. Now I realise it's like eating a bloomin' rainbow and I reckon I've won the pot of gold at the end of it,' he smiled downing another glass of red and rubbing his own protruding pot.

For the rest of the day he bored the best part of the other guests by constantly singing the praises of barbecued vegetables.

'Youse Greeks,' I heard him say to another of m'mates who happened to be a greengrocer, 'with all yer lamb and fatty sausages need a few barbecued vegetables to cut through all that grease.'

Con smiled patiently and listened to an Aussie articulate his first experience with what the Greeks had been doing since before Alexander the Great.

'See this fennel here,' he was told. 'Peter not only uses it with fish, he cuts it up as if it was thin little bits of green straw and sprinkles it over barbecued apple cucumber. Now how's that for an idea, eh? Bet you Greeks hadn't thought of that.'

'No,' answered Con.

'There ya go. What did I tell ya?' was the exuberant reply. 'You can learn something every day, can't you mate? And I'm just the boy to tell ya. Barbecued vegetables? Well that's something new and, I'm telling ya, once you've tried it ya reckon all yer Christmases have come at once.'

'Yeah,' said Con. 'Well, I'd better buy you a drink. Would you like a retsina?'

'What?' gasped m'mate. 'D'ya think I'm a bloody pooftah?'

LATKES
Makes 12

INGREDIENTS

750 g (1½ lb) potatoes (not new ones)
3 eggs, beaten
1 tablespoon plain flour
¼ teaspoon salt
¼ medium onion, grated
75 g (2½ oz) butter
3 tablespoons olive oil

METHOD

- Peel and grate the potatoes, then squeeze them in your hands to get as much water out of them as possible. You should have about 500 g (1 lb) of potato left.
- Put them in a bowl with the eggs then sift in the flour and salt, add the onion, and mix well.
- Put a third of the butter and a tablespoon of the olive oil into a frying pan and heat.
- Divide the potato mixture into half, then each half into thirds, and each of these into half again, so that you have 12 piles of mixture.
- Make each pile into a pancake about 8 cm (3″) in diameter. Fry them on the barbecue hotplate (all at once, if space permits, or in batches). Cook until golden brown.
- Drain on paper towel and keep hot whilst you cook the rest of the meal. Serve hot.

CHINESE SALAD
Serves 4

INGREDIENTS

4 celery stalks
2 small heads Chinese cabbage, shredded
75 g (2½ oz) beanshoots
75 g (2½ oz) snowpeas, sliced diagonally into diamond shapes
½ small red capsicum, seeded and cut into thin rings
75 g (2½ oz) mushrooms, sliced

DRESSING

INGREDIENTS

2 teaspoons lemon juice
1½ tablespoons light soy sauce
¾ teaspoon sesame oil
4 tablespoons sunflower oil
1 teaspoon caster sugar
¼ teaspoon finely chopped fresh root ginger

METHOD

- Mix all the dressing ingredients together, and put on one side to let the flavours develop.
- Slice the celery into horseshoe shapes by laying each stalk flat and slicing it at an angle.
- Put all the ingredients into a large salad bowl, pour the dressing over and toss well.

SALAD ROQUEFORT
Serves 4–6

INGREDIENTS

2 heads of chicory, trimmed and separated into spears
1 iceberg lettuce, shredded
3 celery stalks, sliced
1 Granny Smith apple, peeled, cored and diced

DRESSING

INGREDIENTS

75 g (2½ oz) Roquefort cheese
150 ml (5 fl oz) sour cream
1 teaspoon olive oil
salt
freshly ground black pepper

METHOD

- To make the dressing, mash the cheese with a fork and add the sour cream. Put through a blender, then add the oil, salt and freshly ground black pepper.
- Arrange the chicory around the edge of a large shallow dish, put the lettuce in the centre and sprinkle on the celery and apple.
- Serve with the dressing.

'SEAWEED'

Serves 4

INGREDIENTS

175 g (5½ oz) dark-green, outer leaves of cabbage (cut off thick stem)
peanut oil
1 teaspoon sugar
pinch of salt
25 g (1 oz) slivered almonds

METHOD

- Roll 2 cabbage leaves together into a tight cylinder shape and, using a sharp knife, shred them as finely as possible. Repeat this until all the leaves are shredded.

- Half-fill a wok with oil and heat over a high heat until very hot. Drop in the cabbage and stir for 2 minutes, but don't let it get too dark or it will taste bitter.

- Lift out the cabbage and drain on paper towel then put it on to a warmed serving platter.

- Sprinkle with sugar, salt and slivered almonds, and serve straight away.

APPLE AND ALMOND SALAD
Serves 4

INGREDIENTS

3 Granny Smith apples
lemon juice
175 g (5½ oz) celery, chopped
175 g (5½ oz) tasty cheese, diced
60 g (2 oz) toasted blanched almonds
celery leaves to garnish

DRESSING

INGREDIENTS

150 ml (5 fl oz) natural yoghurt
60 ml (2 fl oz) mayonnaise
2 teaspoons lemon juice
salt
freshly ground black pepper
1 teaspoon chopped fresh parsley

METHOD

- To make the dressing, beat together the yoghurt and mayonnaise, then add the lemon juice, salt, pepper and parsley.
- Core and thinly slice two of the apples — don't peel them. Brush them with lemon juice to prevent them browning.
- Put them into a bowl with the celery, cheese and almonds; pour the dressing over them, and toss.
- Core and thinly slice the remaining apple — again don't peel it. Arrange the slices around the outer edge of a serving dish, pile the dressed salad in the centre and garnish with celery leaves.

Crocodile food

I once had a client who did a contra deal with one of his clients who resided in the north of the Northern Territory. Twice a year, we all decided it was vitally important that we should meet at Channel Point, which is a little-visited area west of Darwin. It's sometimes referred to as the Perron Islands area.

When I say it was not often visited, I exclude the Aborigines from that sweeping remark, for they live and hunt there in what many of us would consider to be an idyllic lifestyle. The Timor Sea husbands an abundance of fish, both shelled and finned. Kangaroos and crocodiles, emus and goannas, all share the bush with buffalo and other edibles. Roots and tubers, nuts and berries, fronds and hearts of palm give those who seek them a balanced healthy diet.

This is when I first met Roy Bigfoot, a huge solid man, who held the respect of his tribe for not only his physical prowess but his mental agility as well. His daughters were healthy, fresh-faced young girls who laughed a lot at life as they helped their mother each day collect food for themselves and anyone who wished to share it with them.

Their mother was a serene woman of small stature but imposing dignity.

'I'd like to try a fresh heart of palm,' I explained to Bigfoot one day as we wandered through the lush tropical growth of the area.

The challenge was accepted, and a home-made stone axe jumped into the powerful hand of Bigfoot. With much grunting, he hacked through a stately palm which crashed into the lily-studded water of a lagoon.

Startled crocodiles blinked their eyes and slid effortlessly from their slumber into the water.

Mrs Bigfoot plunged into the water also, striding knee-deep through its inky blackness. With a knife made from a sharpened file she hacked out the heart of the palm, which is that new-growth area in the centre of the fronds.

'My God!' I gasped to Bigfoot, 'The bloody crocodiles will get her.'

'No, mate,' he laughed. 'With legs as thin as hers, they'll ignore her.'

It is true that the crocodiles left her alone but it is equally true that the missus wasted no time, and it seemed to me that she was attempting to run on top of the water using very large strides.

Although the heart of palm was delicious I was careful, in future, to ask only for food which was entirely crocodile proof.

DEVILLED ARTICHOKES
Serves 4

INGREDIENTS

3 tablespoons walnut oil
1 teaspoon Dijon mustard
1 tablespoon lemon juice
1 tablespoon chopped fresh chervil
salt
freshly ground black pepper
1 lettuce, separated into leaves
175 g (5½ oz) cooked prawns, shelled and de-veined
425 g (13½ oz) artichoke hearts, drained and halved
2 tomatoes, skinned, seeded and chopped*

METHOD

- For the dressing, beat the walnut oil into the mustard, then beat in the lemon juice, chervil, salt and pepper.

- Arrange the lettuce on 4 individual plates, pile the prawns in the centre and the artichoke hearts around the prawns. Scatter the tomatoes over the artichokes.

- Spoon the dressing over the artichoke hearts, and trickle a little over the lettuce too. Serve straight away.

To skin the tomatoes, hold them on a fork over a flame, or drop them into very hot water for a minute or two, until the skin splits and will peel off easily.

ASPARAGUS WITH BUTTER AND BASIL

Serves 1 or more

INGREDIENTS

fresh asparagus
butter
sprinkle of dried basil leaves

METHOD

- Snap the asparagus by holding each end of the asparagus between your thumb and forefinger and bending it down in an arch. The asparagus will snap where the woody part of the stem ends. You can keep the white parts for asparagus soup and the tender ends with the tips are the pieces that you use to cook in the following way.

- Place the asparagus in a frying pan with about 2.5 cm (1") of water. Heat gently until the water is just simmering; by then the asparagus will be cooked. Drain the water out of the pan (you can use this water as a base for a soup).

- Now, pop a couple of dobs of butter into the pan on top of the hot asparagus. Sprinkle some dried basil over it and gently roll the asparagus around until it is covered with the butter and basil sauce. Serve on a warm, but not hot, plate.

CORN ON THE COB WITH BUTTER AND BASIL

Serves 1 or more

INGREDIENTS

1 corn cob per person
nob of butter
sprinkle of dried basil leaves

METHOD

- Peel the husk of the corn back, but don't tear them off. Tear off and throw away the silk. Spread the corn cob with butter, sprinkle with basil leaves, then pull the husks back over the cob to completely cover it.

- Tie at the top with a kitchen-bag tie. Throw on to the barbecue, and cook over hot coals for about 15–20 minutes.

CURRIED POTATO AND ONION
Serves 4

INGREDIENTS

1 large onion
2 tablespoons olive oil
1 teaspoon good Indian curry powder
1½ cups cold boiled potatoes
1 teaspoon French mustard
¼ cup dry sherry
2 tablespoons chopped parsley

METHOD

- Peel the onion and chop it finely. Heat half the oil in a frying pan, stir in the curry powder and then sauté the onion in it until the onion is transparent.
- Meanwhile, slice the potatoes, heat the rest of the oil in another frying pan, stir in the French mustard and then pop in the potato slices and sauté them until they are warmed through.
- Pour in the sherry and sprinkle with parsley. Mix the curried onions with them, and serve very hot.
- This recipe can easily be made on a barbecue hotplate.

TOMATOES AND CAPSICUM

Serves 1 or more

INGREDIENTS

1 capsicum and 1 tomato per person
olive oil

METHOD

- Wash the capsicum and soak in ice water for an hour; then cut into about 2 cm ($^3/_4$") squares, discarding the coarse white membrane. You can eat the seeds if you wish; they're not hot.

- Cook the capsicum in several tablespoons of hot olive oil until soft and slightly browned. Pour off or scrape away all the excess oil and add as much peeled (see page 78) and chopped tomato as there is capsicum.

- Season well with salt and pepper. Push to the back of the hotplate, and cook slowly for 20 to 30 minutes. Serve as a side dish with barbecued meats.

One Big
PICNIC

Picnic in bed

Picnics are meals which are planned and prepared in one place and carried to another.

A picnic is usually shared with ants and other uninvited guests. It is usually eaten in an idyllic spot which nature has fashioned for the purpose of picnicking.

Burke and Wills picnicked on the banks of Cooper Creek, and Captain Phillip, RN, on the sandy beach of Sydney Cove. Sir Edmund Hillary, followed by his son, picnicked on Mt Everest, and Robert the Bruce on a bonnie loch. The uninvited guests were blow-flies, Aborigines, a snowstorm and the Plantagenets.

I had a picnic sitting up in a bed in Kew, a suburb of Melbourne. The food was prepared by Chef Chipolata, then owner of the Latin Restaurant, and delivered by cab to my hospital bed in Kew. You see I was recovering from a minor operation, which in no way was life threatening, except that I was being subjected to the food at this particular hospital.

Being bedridden, I was unable to exercise, and the unimaginative, badly prepared food was a dietitian's nightmare. It sat like concrete in my stomach. I pleaded for fresh fruit and vegetables, less animal fat, as well as cereals and grains, but the private hospital's kitchen couldn't cope, and so I decided to eat alfresco inside.

I refused to eat the food sent to me from their kitchen and, to prove the point, locked the door from the inside at mealtimes.

I rang my friend, Chef Chipolata, told him of my predicament and, within hours, there was a signalled rap on the door. In marched the courier with silver platters bedecked with glittering covers — my picnic.

I'd spread a travelling rug on my bed and scattered it with gum leaves delivered by a sympathetic nurse. Once the plates were arrayed around me and their covers lifted, my stomach applauded what my eyes beheld.

A small fillet of whiting, which had been allowed to go cold, nestled in a couscous flecked with softened seaweed and wet with a splendid fish stock. Lettuce of varying colours and design was served on its own plate. Not quite hidden amongst the leaves were slices of avocado. Sprinkled over the lot were fillets of anchovy which had been soaked in milk to de-salt them. To add even more colour, there were segments of orange which had been meticulously denuded of all pith and the 'skin' which separates the segments. And, of course, there were no pips either. There was also a mixture of macadamia oil, lemon juice, a sprinkle of garlic salt and white pepper; a little raspberry vinegar was splashed in before it was shaken and presented for me to pour over the kaleidoscope of colour.

ASPARAGUS SALAD
Serves 6–8

INGREDIENTS

500 g (1 lb) fresh asparagus, cut into 5 cm (2") pieces
1 small lettuce, torn into bite size pieces
1 cup sliced celery
¼ cup sliced spring onions
½ cup olive oil
2 tablespoons white wine vinegar
2 tablespoons lemon juice
¼ cup finely chopped cooked beetroot
1 hard-boiled egg, finely chopped
1 tablespoon chopped parsley
1 teaspoon paprika
1 teaspoon each: sugar and salt
½ teaspoon dry mustard
4 drops Tabasco sauce

METHOD

- Holding an asparagus spear at each end, bend it until it snaps. It will snap at the point where the 'wood' starts. Repeat with other spears. Keep the woody ends to one side to use for soup at another time. Place the other ends in a frying pan in which you have about 2.5 cm (1") of water.

- Heat gently until the water is just simmering; by then the asparagus will be cooked. Drain the asparagus, and chill.

- Toss the lettuce, celery, spring onions and asparagus into a salad bowl. Combine the remaining ingredients in a jar, pop on a lid, and shake well. Pour over the vegetables, and toss gently.

SALMON MOUSSE

Serves 4–6

INGREDIENTS

1 tablespoon gelatine
¼ cup cold water
2 teaspoons sugar
1 teaspoon salt
1 teaspoon dry mustard
¼ cup white vinegar
2 cups canned red salmon, drained
1 cup finely chopped celery
2 teaspoons capers
½ cup whipped pure cream

METHOD

• Soak the gelatine in the water for 2 minutes. Add the sugar, salt, mustard and vinegar. Stir over low heat until gelatine has dissolved. Cool in a bowl in the fridge until it is like egg white.

• Fold in salmon, celery and capers. Place in wetted mould until well set. Turn out when set and serve with the following accompaniment.

• Blend 1 teaspoon finely chopped onion, ½ teaspoon salt, ½ cup sour cream, 1 teaspoon horseradish, 2 teaspoons vinegar.

PORK RILLETTES
Serves 8

INGREDIENTS

1.5 kg (3 lb) boneless lean pork
1 teaspoon salt
1 teaspoon pepper
1 clove garlic, crushed
½ teaspoon dried thyme leaves
1 bay leaf
½ cup dry white wine
½ cup water
½ cup unsalted butter

METHOD

- Cut the pork into 3 cm (1¼") cubes. Place the meat into a large casserole and add the salt and pepper, garlic, thyme, bay leaf, white wine and water. Cover tightly, and bake in the oven at 120°C (250°F) for about 4 hours until the meat is so tender it falls apart in shreds when prodded with a fork.

- Discard the bay leaf. Drain and reserve the juices. Let the meat cool then, with 2 forks, shred the pork.

- Let the juices cool, then skim and discard the fat. With a heavy spoon, or your hands, work together the meat, juices and unsalted butter until well blended.

- Spoon into a bowl or pack into a crock or terrine. Cover, and pop in the fridge until you are ready to use it. Serve at room temperature. This will keep in the fridge for a week, or can be frozen.

- Use as sandwich fillings or for open-faced sandwiches, or scoop out and serve as a first course, or even as a light entrée.

Sushi

Seasoned Sushi Rice (Shari)
Serves 4

Ingredients

150 g (5 oz) short grain rice, rinsed and drained
200 ml (6 fl oz) water
8 cm (3") piece kombu seaweed
4 teaspoons rice vinegar

Method

- Put the water, rice and and seaweed in a saucepan, and leave to soak for 15 minutes.
- Pop on a lid and bring to the boil. Simmer until tender, about 10 minutes.
- Leave to cool with the lid on. When cool take out the seaweed and stir in the rice vinegar.

Thin Egg Crepes (Usu Yaki Tamago)
Serves 4

Ingredients

2 eggs	¼ teaspoon salt
1 tablespoon sake	1 ½ teaspoons water
1 ½ teaspoons sugar	olive oil for frying

Method

- Mix together the eggs, sake, sugar, salt and water until they are evenly blended. Let the foam settle.
- Over a gentle heat, pour half the mixture into a lightly oiled 20 cm (8") frying pan, and swirl to evenly coat the base of the pan. Cook until the edges of the crepe begin to dry out. Take the pan off the heat, cool the crepe slightly until you can turn it over. Put the pan back on the heat and cook the other side for about half a minute.

- Slide the crepe from the pan and let it cool whilst you make the second crepe. Use a sharp knife to cut each crepe into a rectangle. Keep the trimmings to shred and use in other sushi.

TIED GOLDEN ROLLS
Makes 8

INGREDIENTS

¼ quantity of Seasoned Sushi Rice
1 teaspoon toasted sesame seeds
½ teaspoon grated fresh root ginger
1 teaspoon rice vinegar
1 teaspoon sugar
2 Thin Egg Crepes, trimmed into rectangles
100 g (3 oz) smoked salmon, cut into long strips

METHOD

- Mix together the rice, sesame seeds, ginger, vinegar and sugar. Then, with wet hands, shape into 2 even rolls the same length as the egg crepes.
- Place each roll on an egg crepe and roll up carefully. Tie 4 strips of smoked salmon along the length of each roll at regular intervals, then chill until you're ready to use them. To serve, cut each roll into 4 pieces between the smoked salmon.

CRAB AND AVOCADO ROLLS
Makes 8

INGREDIENTS

½ ripe avocado (about 100 g/3 oz), peeled and mashed
½ teaspoon wasabi powder
2 teaspoons mayonnaise
salt
5 crab sticks
lemon juice
¼ quantity Seasoned Sushi Rice
2 sheets nori seaweed

METHOD

- Mix together the avocado, wasabi and mayonnaise, then season to taste with salt and lemon juice.
- Sprinkle the crab sticks with lemon juice. Roll the rice into 2 even rolls the length of the nori seaweed.
- Place a sheet of nori on a workbench, preferably on a sudare mat. Arrange a roll of rice at one end, spread half the avocado mixture along the length of the rice and then put 2½ crab sticks along the length of the nori. Roll up carefully, using the sudare mat.
- Repeat with the remaining ingredients. Chill until you're about to use them, then cut each roll into 4 pieces.

SALMON AND DILL HAND ROLLS
Makes 8

INGREDIENTS

2 sheets nori seaweed
¼ quantity Seasoned Sushi Rice
50 g (1½ oz) smoked salmon, cut into 8 pieces
8 slices cucumber, cut into julienne strips
8 sprigs fresh dill
1 teaspoon wasabi powder mixed with 1 teaspoon water
lemon juice

METHOD

- Cut each piece of nori seaweed into 4 squares and lay them out on a workbench. Divide the rice between each, placing it on a corner of the nori.
- Top the rice with a piece of salmon, cucumber, dill and wasabi and sprinkle with lemon juice.
- Fold up the diagonally opposite corner of the seaweed to half cover the filling. Roll the seaweed up into a cone shape, damping the edge if necessary to seal. Chill until ready to serve.

PRAWN SUSHI
Serves 4

INGREDIENTS

¼ quantity of Seasoned Sushi Rice
½ teaspoon wasabi powder mixed with ½ teaspoon water
4 large cooked prawns, shelled
soy sauce

METHOD

- Shape the sushi rice into 4 ovals, sprinkle with a little wasabi and top each with a prawn. Chill until ready to serve.
- Serve with soy sauce for dipping.

The Willy-Willy

Eat tomatoes and you're a goner, it was once believed. Just look at their colour — bright red — which everybody knows is the colour of danger. The *pomme de terre* (the apple of the earth) is marvellous, but not the *pomme de Moore* (the apple of the Moors) with its colour of death.

Those mad Spanish conquistadors brought them back from South America after they'd done over Montezuma and a few of his maidens.

The world studiously ignored the tomato, named after the South American Indians' name for it: *tomatl*. But that name was ignored and the fruit (for that's what it is, not a vegetable) continued to be called the *pomme de Moore*. But a lot of French folks misheard the name. They thought it was referred to as the *pomme d'amour* (the apple of love) and so bought it by the bucketful.

Now I'm told that the tomato is the world's most eaten fruit. From those first tomatoes that the Spanish conquistadors brought back from South America other varieties have been developed, and it's hardly a proper picnic if one of these varieties of tomatoes is not prominent amongst the array of food which seems to appear like magic from picnic baskets and hampers.

Once a spot has been selected under a shady tree or on the bank of a picturesque river, fires crackle into life to lightly char chops and the ubiquitous spud. Potatoes protected by foil are rolled into the ashes. Salads of every description pop on to blankets spread over grass, and tables suddenly become laden with bottles of pickles, sauces, soft drinks and wines.

Plump tomatoes are sliced, sprinkled with oil, herbs and spices. Merriment abounds before, during and after the food fills the tummies of all present.

The average Aussie picnic is in progress.

But I once attended one which was less poetic.

My family drove their old 1924 black DeSotto to the banks of the Tumut River. They'd selected a delightful picnic spot where the river gurgled past waving willows and a stately elm with a girth even greater than my grandmother and grandfather combined.

We all participated in erecting a three-sided tent and unfolding card tables on which to arrange our food. We lit a fire in an area provided after collecting enough wood to fuel the whole of the Inquisition's bonfires.

We toasted thick slices of high-tinned white bread, and let them cool before buttering them. We sliced tomato and sprinkled it with fresh basil while Father carefully turned not-too-thick slices of steak over the glowing coals and flickering flame from his fire.

'We need a bit more huff and puff on the fire,' the old boy suggested.

And believe me, just as he expressed that hope, a strong gust of wind rattled through the trees and scattered the barbecue's coals out over the grass. Immediately, a stronger huff flattened the tent and an even stronger puff lifted the card tables with all their food and drinks high into the air and off over the countryside.

My recollection is confused, as the trauma created by the wind caused everybody not only to scream and wave their hands frantically, but also to run around in circles.

The wind became more intense and, in panic, the family jumped into the car to escape what was obviously the eye of a willy-willy — one of those funnels of wind that roar around in a circle and which the Americans call 'twisters'.

The family fled but forgot me. Some way down the track it was recognised that I was not screaming my lungs out in the back of the car. They turned round and beat their way back to find me hanging on to the fly of the tent and being flapped about as a flag would on the cone of the moon shuttle.

Fortunately the fly was anchored to a huge elm, otherwise I would probably have been blown to billy-o.

Nothing was left of our picnic save a bag of tomatoes which had somehow become wedged in the roots of the ancient elm. The calico bag they were in saved them from the fate of the rest of our feast. Mind you, they were squashed to a pulp.

Our picnic area had been devastated, yet very little damage had been done to the rest of the area as the willy-willy had roared down the river, leaped up over the bank, caused its fun and merriment with our meal and then swooped off down the river again.

That evening, in high excitement, we discussed our escape as we ate our tomato soup. And here's the recipe my mum made.

TOMATO SOUP
Serves 6

INGREDIENTS

8 large tomatoes
2 tablespoons butter
2 slices onion
2 tablespoons plain flour
½ bay leaf
good pinch of dried thyme
2 whole cloves
2 cups water
salt
grated Parmesan cheese

METHOD

- Skin the tomatoes by holding them over a flame on the end of a fork, or dropping them in hot water until the skins split and come off easily.

- Cut the tomatoes in half, hold them cut side down over a strainer and squeeze gently to remove the seeds. Chop the tomatoes.

- Melt the butter in a deep heavy saucepan, add the onion and cook until soft. Stir in the flour and cook until it bubbles.

- Add the chopped tomatoes, bay leaf, thyme and cloves, and simmer until the tomato is soft. Add the water, a little salt and cook for 20 minutes.

- Pop the lot into a blender, then return to the pan to reheat. Serve topped with grated Parmesan cheese.

BACON-WRAPPED TOMATOES
Serves 6

INGREDIENTS
12 bacon rashers
6 medium tomatoes
1 tablespoon brown sugar
1 tablespoon prepared mustard
pinch of salt
toothpicks
aluminium foil

METHOD

• Fry the bacon on foil or a hotplate over hot coals until partially cooked but not crisp.

• Peel the tomatoes by holding them on a fork over a flame or dropping them in hot water until the skins split and come off easily. .

• Mix together the brown sugar, mustard and salt. Make a vertical cut down the centre of each tomato, about $2/3$ of the way through. Spread the cut edges with mustard mixture.

• Criss-cross 2 bacon rashers. Place a tomato on the bacon where the slices cross, bring the strips to the top of the tomato and secure with toothpicks. Place the tomatoes on the foil and seal. Cook over coals until the tomatoes are hot.

From The
KITCHEN
TO THE COUNTRYSIDE

Cold cuts

Ghenghis Khan was born in 1176 or so. If I'm wrong, don't take me to task because it's not that important to this story. Anyway, whenever it was, he grew up, put a rather fearsome army together and galloped out of Mongolia to conquer a goodly part of the known world at that time. And let me tell you, dear reader, that was not an easy job.

There were all sorts of opposition to his effrontery; nevertheless, as a warrior, he and his mob were formidable. They galloped for however long it took to take them to the territory they wished to conquer.

There were no administration hangers-on as we have in our modern armies of today. Every member of his troupe was a fighting man who rode a stallion and trailed behind him several mares. They didn't carry cooks in the entourage, instead they nicked the veins of their horse and drank its blood. They also drank the milk of the mares, which kept them in constant supply of vitamin C enriched milk.

I'm told that mares' milk is far more vitamin C prolific than human milk and that was the reason they didn't suffer from scurvy. No lemons or limes like Captain Cook and his Jack Tars, simply mares' milk and blood. But when a mare died from old age or accident, or if there was an over-abundance of foals born, a throat was cut and the meat frozen simply by allowing it to remain in the snow of the windswept steppes over which the Mongolians marauded.

Now that's really cold cuts.

To thaw out their meat, they put slabs of it under their saddles, and then galloped to their next destination. The meat, pounded by the hard wooden saddles, weighed down by the muscular bottoms of the Mongolians, defrosted and tenderised, thereby inventing steak tartare.

The Tartar warriors served their mashed meat raw with whatever they could scavenge from the countryside, which in most cases wasn't much.

Our history of cold cuts seems more civilised.

The family roast was carved at the table and eaten with the vegetables cooked in the roasting pan juices. Green marble peas were practically a must, as was gravy and a slice of bread which was liberally buttered. But it's the next day and the day after that I'm now talking of, because it was then that the cold cuts of roast beef or leg of lamb were eaten, and many thought that they were tastier cold than they were when they were served hot.

Most Aussie children of the 1940s, 50s and 60s well remember the cold roast sandwiches in their school lunch-box and the absolutely delicious congealed jelly and crisp fat which sometimes clung to the edges of the offering.

Well, my friends, if it was so good then, what has changed? The answer is — nothing.

Roasts shouldn't be a thing of the past and nor should be the cold cuts which are served in their aftermath.

There is a marvellous array of chutneys and pickles which are made commercially, the purchase price of which is, in my opinion, eminently reasonable. But there are those clever ones amongst us who have the expertise and the time to make their own. And, in my opinion, one shouldn't sneer at the cold cuts sandwich.

There are some magnificent breads available, either bought from the boutique bakeries or made in one's own oven or those new fangled, whiz-bang, you-beaut breadmaking machines which have become so popular.

STEAK TARTARE
Serves 1

INGREDIENTS

1 piece of eye fillet of beef
1 egg yolk
1 tablespoon finely chopped onion
6 capers
1 tablespoon horseradish
1 tablespoon good French mustard
1 tablespoon caviar

METHOD

- Trim the beef of all pieces of fat and sinew. It must be eye fillet of beef, and it must be at room temperature.

- With the sharp edge of a dessertspoon or a not-so-sharp knife, scrape the beef until it comes away on your knife or spoon as a soft pulp. DON'T MINCE IT!

- Form the scraped beef into a little mound in the centre of a plate. Make a hollow in the centre of the mound and drop in the yolk of an egg without breaking it so that it sits there as if in a nest.

- Place a little chopped onion, the capers, horseradish, French mustard, and caviar into individual small dishes or ramekins, and surround the meat dish with them.

- Each person prepares their own tartare by mixing all the ingredients from the ramekins together, taking as much of the flavours as they like to suit their taste.

Summer Terrine
Serves 4

Ingredients

100 g (3 oz) small French beans, trimmed
100 g (3 oz) peas
175 g (5½ oz) young carrots, cut in lengthways strips
100 g (3 oz) young spinach leaves
500 g (1 lb) cream cheese
2 eggs, lightly beaten
finely grated rind of half a lemon
1 garlic clove, crushed
25 g (1 oz) ham, minced
salt
freshly ground black pepper
6 artichoke hearts, drained and diced

Method

- Boil the beans, peas and carrots separately until they're just tender; then drain them and pour cold water over them to stop them cooking further. Blanch the spinach leaves for about half a minute.

- Line a 1 kg (2 lb) loaf tin with the spinach leaves, overlapping the edges. Beat the cheese until it has softened, then gradually beat in the eggs, lemon rind, garlic, ham, salt and pepper.

- Put a layer of the cheese mixture into the tin, then a layer of beans, a layer of cheese mixture, a layer of carrots, another layer of cheese mixture, a layer of artichokes, a layer of cheese mixture and a layer of peas. Finish with a layer of cheese mixture.

- Fold the spinach leaves over the filling to enclose it, cover with foil, and put it in a roasting dish. Pour boiling water into the dish to come halfway up the loaf tin, then bake in the oven at 160°C (325°F) for 40 minutes.

- Take it out of the oven, let it cool completely, and chill overnight or for at least 4 hours. Turn out of the loaf tin, garnish with lemon slices, and serve.

STUFFED VINE LEAVES

Serves 6–8

INGREDIENTS

100 g (3 oz) long grain rice
225 g (7 oz) minced beef
25 g (1 oz) pine kernels
25 g (1 oz) currants
150 g (5 oz) spring onions,
    finely chopped
3 tablespoons chopped parsley
1 tablespoon dried mint
¼ teaspoon ground allspice
¼ teaspoon ground cinnamon

2 tablespoons tomato purée
salt
freshly ground black pepper
500 g (1 lb) vine leaves*
3 large garlic cloves, slivered
150 ml (5 fl oz) olive oil
150 ml (5 fl oz) water
juice of 2 lemons
1 teaspoon sugar

If using fresh vine leaves, soak them in boiling water until limp. If using canned leaves, pour off the brine and cover the leaves with boiling water. Leave them to soak for 20 minutes, drain and rinse under cold water.

METHOD

- Pour boiling water over the rice, soak for 20 minutes, then drain well. Mix together the beef, pine kernels, currants, spring onions, parsley, mint, allspice, cinnamon, tomato purée, salt and pepper, then add the drained rice. Choose the larger vine leaves for stuffing and use the smaller, damaged leaves to line the base and sides of a medium-sized flameproof dish or casserole.

- Place one vine leaf at a time, vein-side up, on the workbench and snip off the stalk. Put about a tablespoon of filling near the centre of the stem. Fold the sides over, and roll the leaf into a small rectangular parcel. If the leaves are too small, place one leaf over another, halfway down, and roll as one.

- Pack the parcels tightly into the prepared dish, pushing the slivers of garlic in between them. Mix together the olive oil, water, lemon juice and sugar, and pour over the stuffed leaves. Put a small plate on the top to prevent the leaves from unravelling during cooking. Bring to the boil, lower the heat, cover the dish, and simmer gently for 2 hours.

- Serve either hot or cold with natural yoghurt.

LAMB AND EGG BALLS
Makes 12

INGREDIENTS

6 hard-boiled eggs
2 spring onions
280 g (9 oz) cooked lamb
1 tablespoon chopped chives
mayonnaise
½ cup chopped walnuts

METHOD

- Chop the eggs and spring onions, and mince the lamb. Mix them all together with the chives, and add enough mayonnaise to just bind them.
- Divide the mixture into 12, and roll each portion into a ball. Roll very lightly in chopped walnuts, then put the balls on grease-proof paper into the fridge to chill.
- Serve with a crisp green salad.

VEAL AND RABBIT MOULD
Serves 4

INGREDIENTS

4 eggs
2 teaspoons cornflour
freshly ground black pepper
1¾ cups warm milk
250 g (8 oz) cooked veal
60 g (2 oz) cooked rabbit
salt
1 tablespoon gelatin
3 tablespoons warm water
½ cup fresh cream
watercress, cucumber and tomato for garnish

METHOD

- Separate the eggs, and whisk the egg yolks and cornflour together with a little pepper. Now, beat in the warm milk, and pour the mixture into the top of a double boiler (or a bowl over a saucepan of simmering water), stirring all the time until it's thick enough to coat the spoon you're stirring with.

- Stir in the minced veal and rabbit, and a little salt. Next, dissolve the gelatine in the warm water, and gradually stir it into the mixture. Pop the whole lot into the fridge until it is almost set. While you are waiting, beat the egg whites until they are stiff, and whip the cream until it starts to thicken. Fold them both into the chilled veal and rabbit mixture.

- Brush a mould with a little olive oil, pour in the veal and rabbit mixture, and put it back in the fridge to chill and set. When it is ready, unmould it on to a serving platter, and garnish with watercress, strips of cucumber and tomato rings.

FISH MOULD
Serves 4

INGREDIENTS

450 g (14½ oz) cooked, flaked fish
300 ml (10 fl oz) bechamel sauce (see below)
2 eggs, well beaten
150 ml (5 fl oz) cream
2 tablespoons finely chopped chives
2 tablespoons finely chopped parsley
salt and pepper

METHOD

- Mix the flaked fish with the bechamel sauce, add the beaten eggs, cream, chives, parsley, salt and pepper. Put into a buttered mould, and stand it in a baking tin of hot water. Cook in the oven at 200°C (400°F) for 30 minutes. Chill, turn out and serve with a piquant sauce.

BECHAMEL SAUCE

INGREDIENTS

40 g (1½ oz) butter   40 g (1½ oz) plain flour
600 ml (20 fl oz) milk   salt and pepper

METHOD

- Melt the butter in a heavy saucepan over low heat. Stir in the flour with a wooden spoon. In another pan have ready the milk heated to boiling point. Take the butter and flour off the heat and very slowly pour in the boiling milk, stirring fast and always in the same direction. Still stirring, put the pan back over the heat until it boils. Turn the heat down, put a lid on to prevent a skin forming and let it simmer for another 15 minutes.

- Season with salt and pepper, and it is ready for using in any recipe calling for bechamel sauce.

MEATLOAF
Serves 8–10

INGREDIENTS

1 tablespoon butter
750 g (1½ lb) minced beef
125 g (4 oz) minced pork shoulder
½ cup boiled rice (or breadcrumbs soaked in milk)
1 large onion, grated
1 large carrot, grated
1 clove garlic, crushed
2 eggs
¼ cup orange juice
1 tablespoon finely chopped parsley
good pinch paprika
2 drops Tabasco sauce
freshly ground black pepper

METHOD

- Melt the butter, then mix in all the remaining ingredients.
- Place the mixture in a loaf tin, and pop it in the oven at 190°C (375°F) for about 45 minutes, or until it's brown and set. Let the loaf cool in the tin, then turn it out and slice it.

MOCK EMU EGGS
Makes 4

INGREDIENTS

6 flat anchovy fillets
125 g (4 oz) minced ham
1 cup soft fresh breadcrumbs
couple of drops Tabasco sauce
1 egg, beaten
4 hard-boiled eggs, shelled
dry breadcrumbs for coating
olive oil for deep frying

METHOD

- Chop the anchovies very finely and add to the minced ham, together with the breadcrumbs and the Tabasco sauce. Bind them together with the beaten egg.

- Now put a good thick coating of this mixture over each hard-boiled egg, which should be cold. Then coat them with the dry breadcrumbs. Press the breadcrumbs on firmly.

- Pop the eggs into hot oil for about 7 minutes. To test the heat of the oil, drop in a soft breadcrumb and in 40 seconds it should turn golden brown. When the eggs are cooked, take them from the oil, drain them on paper towel and allow them to cool.

SMOKED TROUT PÂTÉ
Serves 6–8

INGREDIENTS

2 x 500 g (1 lb) trout, smoked
125 g (4 oz) butter
freshly ground black pepper
juice of 1 lemon
2 tablespoons thickened cream
a good pinch of nutmeg

METHOD

- Skin the trout and take the flesh off the bone. Mash a little butter into the trout flesh, then put the fish, all the butter, pepper, lemon juice, cream and nutmeg into a blender and purée until it is a smooth paste.

- Spoon the pâté into pots, cover tightly with foil, and pop into the fridge until you're ready to use it. It will keep for about 5 days.

- Serve with slices of hot crusty bread.

Alfresco
ON PATIOS
AND BALCONIES

Les, we love you

There's not a lot to tell about Les, other than he was a little kid with freckles and fire-red hair. He had a cheeky grin and a tooth missing, blue eyes that squinted at you in the sun, and a knee which was inevitably grazed and was a short distance above socks which seemed to coil around his ankles.

Everyone loved Les, whose real name was Jamie. His family and friends nicknamed him Les because of his constant, 'Les go down to the river for a swim. Les try and get money for an ice-cream from Mum,' or les do this or les do that or les do the other.

Les loved life and just about everything else but spaghetti which, cruelly, it seemed to me, his mother from time to time served him despite his pleas, of, 'Les have something else — like a hamburger or a pizza, eh?'

I suspect that Les's mum served it because of the ingenious way he disposed of it. And that wasn't down his cake-hole.

When Les was assured the family's attention was diverted to something else happening around the table, he would shovel a forkful of the tomato-sauce-covered spaghetti into the top of his voluminous sock. When he considered one sock to be full to capacity with the slippery pasta he'd start on the second sock. Once that sock was full he'd excuse himself from the table on the pretext of going to the toilet where, instead of emptying his bladder, he'd empty his socks.

It's amazing that Les believed nobody heard the squelch, squelch, squelch of his exit, but he must have, as every spaghetti night was a repeat performance.

Mind you, I must disclose I don't blame the lad because the spaghetti was tinned. Maybe if it had been otherwise Les may have approved of the following suggestions. And especially if they'd been served outdoors where he could have disposed of the offering more easily if, in fact, my summation of his approval was incorrect.

SPAGHETTI WITH BACON AND TOMATO SAUCE
Serves 4

INGREDIENTS

¼ cup olive oil
1 onion, thinly sliced
220 g (7 oz) rindless bacon, cut into short julienne strips
1 kg (2 lb) ripe tomatoes, finely chopped
salt
¼ cup small fresh basil leaves
freshly ground black pepper
500 g (1 lb) spaghetti
90 g (3oz) grated Pecorino cheese

METHOD

- Heat the oil in a saucepan over moderate heat, add the onion and bacon and brown for 10 minutes.

- Add the tomatoes and a little salt, and simmer, covered, over very low heat for 1 hour. Just before removing the sauce from the heat, add the whole basil leaves and a good pinch of pepper.

- Cook the spaghetti in boiling salted water until *al dente* (still has a little bite to it), then drain. Serve topped with the sauce and sprinkled with the cheese.

YELLOW AND GREEN NOODLES WITH CREAM, HAM AND MUSHROOM SAUCE
Serves 4

INGREDIENTS

90 g (3 oz) butter

2 tablespoons finely chopped onion

350 g (11 oz) mushrooms, cut into 6 mm (¼") cubes

salt

freshly ground black pepper

175 g (4 oz) ham, cut into fine strips

180 ml (6 fl oz) cream

200 g (6½ oz) fettuccine

200 g (6½ oz) spinach fettuccine

50 g (1½ oz) freshly grated Parmesan cheese

METHOD

- Place half the butter into a large heavy frying pan, and add the onion. Sauté over a medium heat until the onion starts to turn golden, then turn the heat up a little and add the mushrooms. After the mushrooms have absorbed all the butter, add the salt and pepper, and shake the pan, moving and tossing the mushrooms. When the mushroom juice appears, cook for about 3 minutes, stirring often.

- Turn the heat down, add the ham and cook it for half a minute, still stirring. Add half the cream and cook until the cream thickens. Take the pan off the heat and keep on one side.

- Using a flameproof serving dish, heat the rest of the butter and cream over a low heat. When the butter is melted into the cream turn off the heat and keep on one side.

- Cook the fettuccine in salted boiling water, dropping the spinach fettuccine into the water a few minutes after the yellow, as it cooks quicker. Don't overcook the fettuccine as it will continue to soften when cooking with the sauce. Drain the fettuccine, and drop it into the serving dish with the cream and butter.

- Place the flameproof dish over a low heat and toss in the fettuccine to coat it with the cream and butter. Stir in half the mushroom sauce and the grated cheese. Take off the heat. Pour the rest of the mushroom sauce into a hollow in the centre of the mound of fettuccine. Serve with an extra bowl of cheese alongside.

FETTUCCINE WITH EGGPLANT AND ANCHOVY
Serves 4

INGREDIENTS

6 tomatoes
olive oil
½ eggplant, peeled and coarsely chopped
2 capsicum, chopped
2 cloves garlic, crushed
4 anchovy fillets
1 tablespoon capers
2 teaspoons chopped fresh basil leaves
freshly ground black pepper
12 black olives, pitted
500 g (1 lb) fettuccine

METHOD

- Peel the tomatoes by holding them over a gas flame on the end of a fork, or drop them into very hot water for a minute or two, until the skin splits and peels off easily.

- Heat the oil in a large, heavy-base frying pan and throw in the tomatoes, eggplant, capsicum and garlic. Simmer over a medium heat until the eggplant is cooked.

- Chop the anchovy fillets, and toss them into the pan, together with the capers and basil. Sprinkle with a little freshly ground black pepper and the black olives. Stir and leave over a low heat while you cook the fettuccine.

- Drop the fettuccine into 4 litres (7 pints) of salted boiling water, and bring back to boil. Simmer until the fettuccine is cooked but still a little firm.

- Drain thoroughly, and pile into a warm serving bowl. Mix the eggplant sauce through, and serve.

ITALIAN-STYLE WINTER SOUP
Serves 10–12

INGREDIENTS

1 large onion, finely chopped
2 cloves crushed garlic
olive oil
1 green capsicum, chopped
500 g (1 lb) minced lean steak
1 litre (1¾ pints) bean stock
30 g (1 oz) tomato paste
2 x 410 g (13 oz) cans peeled chopped tomatoes
1 teaspoon dried basil
pinch of dried oregano
125 g (4 oz) finely chopped hot salami
2 chopped zucchini
½ small packet frozen peas
salt
freshly ground black pepper

METHOD

- Fry the onion and garlic gently in a little oil. Add the capsicum, and cook a little longer. Remove this mixture from the pan.
- Brown the meat. Drain off any excess fat. Return the vegetable mixture to the pan, add the stock, tomato paste, tomatoes, herbs and salami. Simmer about 15 minutes, then add the zucchini and peas, and cook a further few minutes. Small pastas can be added before zucchini and peas.
- Serve with crusty bread and grated Parmesan cheese.

FRENCH BEANS WITH HAZELNUT DRESSING
Serves 4

INGREDIENTS

500 g (1 lb) French beans, trimmed
150 ml (5 fl oz) sour cream
75 ml (2½ fl oz) mayonnaise
juice of half a lemon
salt
75 g (2½ oz) hazelnuts
lemon slices to garnish

METHOD

- Cook the French beans by dropping them into boiling water for only a few minutes so that they retain their crunch and colour. Don't cook them too long.

- Beat the sour cream and mayonnaise together, then gradually beat in the lemon juice, and add salt to taste.

- Put the hazelnuts on a baking tray and pop them into a hot oven for a few minutes until they start to colour — don't let them get too dark. Rub them in a tea towel to take off the skins, then chop them roughly.

- Arrange the French beans on individual dishes, spoon the dressing over the beans, sprinkle with hazelnuts and garnish with lemon slices.

Roasted Rabbit with Tarragon
Serves 4

Ingredients

2 tablespoons olive oil
1 onion, finely chopped
4 rashers rindless bacon
4 pieces rabbit (about 250 g/8 oz each)
300 ml (10 fl oz) dry cider
1 tablespoon fresh chopped tarragon or 1 teaspoon dried tarragon
2 tablespoons honey
1 tablespoon Dijon mustard
2 apples, peeled, cored and cut into 8 pieces
1 tablespoon cornflour
2 tablespoons water
1 teaspoon tomato purée
salt
freshly ground black pepper
fresh tarragon springs to garnish

Method

- Oil the base of a roasting dish with some of the oil. Throw in the chopped onion. Wrap a slice of bacon around each piece of rabbit and secure it with a toothpick. Put the rabbit on top of the onion, and roast at 230°C (475°F) for 45 minutes.

- Mix together the cider, chopped tarragon, honey and mustard, and pour it over the rabbit. Cover, and continue to cook, lowering the temperature to 180°C (350°F) for an hour.

- Fry the apples in the remaining oil until they are golden brown. Take the rabbit from the roasting dish, take out and discard the toothpicks and keep the rabbit hot.

- Pour the pan juices over the apples. Dissolve the cornflour in the water, and stir it into the pan; then simmer gently, stirring all the time, until the sauce thickens. Stir in the tomato purée and season to taste. Pour the sauce over the rabbit, and garnish with tarragon sprigs.

VEAL MEATBALLS IN A SOUR CREAM AND CAPER SAUCE

Serves 4

INGREDIENTS

500 g (1 lb) minced lean veal
1 small onion, finely chopped
1 tablespoon chopped parsley
salt
freshly ground black pepper
pinch of nutmeg
50 g (1½ oz) white breadcrumbs, fresh
1 egg, lightly beaten
seasoned flour
2 tablespoons olive oil
4 tablespoons white wine
1 tablespoon capers, drained
150 ml (5 fl oz) sour cream
chopped parsley to garnish

METHOD

- Mix together the veal, onion, parsley, salt, pepper, nutmeg and breadcrumbs, then mix in the lightly beaten egg. Shape the mixture into 16 oval balls, and toss them in the seasoned flour.

- Heat the oil in a large frying pan, and cook the meatballs for 15 minutes or until they're evenly browned and cooked through. Take them from the pan with a slotted spoon, and keep them hot whilst you make the sauce.

- Pour off half the oil from the pan, then add the wine, scraping the base of the pan to loosen any bits stuck to it. Bring to the boil. Lower the heat, and stir in the capers and sour cream. Heat gently but don't boil. Adjust the seasonings to your taste. Arrange the meatballs on a warmed serving platter, pour the sauce over the top, and sprinkle with parsley.

LAMB WITH QUINCE, GINGER AND LEMON
Serves 6

INGREDIENTS

2 tablespoons olive oil
1 small onion, finely chopped
1.5 kg (3 lb) shoulder of lamb
½ teaspoon finely chopped fresh root ginger
salt
freshly ground black pepper
450 ml (15 fl oz) water
¼ teaspoon saffron powder
500 g (1 lb) quinces, peeled, cored and sliced
juice of ½ lemon

METHOD

- Heat the oil in a large flameproof casserole, or pot with a lid, and fry the onion until it is soft.
- Trim the fat from the underside of the lamb, then add it to the casserole and brown it all over.
- Stir in the ginger, add salt and pepper, and the water and saffron. Bring to the boil, cover, and simmer for 2 hours.
- Drop in the sliced quinces and add the lemon juice. Continue to simmer until the quinces are tender (about 30 minutes). Serve with steamed rice.

Half-a-second diet

My half-a-second diet is — 'don't'.

Most diets are dangerous and dopey, designed by dubious doctors who threaten to decrease your waistline whilst they expand their wallet.

Magazine editors instruct a staff personality to 'prepare a diet to welcome summer, or winter, or spring or autumn for that matter, and shrink a tummy or two whilst we expand our readership.' The fact that the columnist has no expertise in formulating a diet causes not a ripple of concern amongst the editorial staff, but it should amongst the magazine's readers.

Australia's senior nutritionists have damned most magazine diets as not only dopey, but downright dangerous.

Most dietitians agree that we should eat a variety of food, concentrating on cereals, fruit and vegetables. We are told to limit our animal fat intake but not to avoid fats altogether. For instance, if you butter a piece of bread, don't top it with cheese. Or if you have cream in a main course sauce, don't have cream on a dessert.

We should not constantly eat deep-fried foods, but not sink into a fit of depression if we eat a chip or two. A thick-cut potato chip, with its skin on and browned in olive oil, can be delicious. We know the potato is good for us and the oil of fruit seems to have done the Italians no harm at all. But that doesn't mean we eat a chaffbag full of them.

Nevertheless, you can consume large portions of the right food cooked sensibly and still not end up like Billy or Betty Bunter. It is when we eat only fat-saturated and fried foods that we come to grief. For instance, consider an antipasto consisting of salamis and other sausages, which are made up of chunks of pure fat holding together minuscule pieces of meat, followed by a cream-enriched soup, a cheese-and-herb-stuffed cannelloni with a cream-based sauce, a rich chocolate cake with whipped brandy cream or cream-filled brandy snaps, finished off with a cheese platter. Much better would be sundried tomatoes, artichoke hearts with sardines, followed by a consommé of chicken broth with puréed beetroot, poached fish with an orange and garlic sauce, an array of colour-coded vegetables, followed by a cheese, dried fruit and nuts course, and, to complete the meal, blueberries and orange segments in a fruit juice and wine sauce.

I don't believe in dieting but I do believe that we should all be aware of what we eat and, of course, we should exercise daily. Walk upstairs rather than catch a lift. Walk to the shops rather than drive a car. Play a game of tennis rather than lie down for the afternoon. You know the sort of thing I mean.

But let's get back to being constantly aware of what we eat.

The colour combination of vegetables makes choosing them easy and eating them pleasant. An orange carrot with a green leaf vegetable, a yellow squash and a white potato means we are getting

a good range of vitamins and minerals. Fish one day and steak the next. Mixed-bean pies with a puréed tomato sauce surrounded with flowerets of broccoli and cauliflower make a marvellous meal without meat. So the next day we can eat a grilled lamb chop or a chargrilled steak.

Breakfast should be fruit and cereal, and lunch a sandwich without butter.

I've heard it said that when we diet one week and not the next, our bodies, which are designed to adjust to this on-and-off food intake, do just that — they compensate for the over-feeding one minute, under-feeding the next. They subtract fat from the food and store it in fat cells, waiting for the next 'drought'. So, though we may diet for a week or more, our bodies jealously guard our fat build-up in case the 'drought' goes on for months. So a diet causes us to lose a little weight at the start (that's before the body wakes up to what's going on and hangs on to its stored fat like a squirrel does with acorns). When we break the diet, even though we still have fats in reserve, our body hoards more, just in case.

So these diets simply warn our body that hard times could be round the corner, and it had better take defensive measures. Therefore it is much better to have a regular feeding pattern which supplies the body with the essential nutrients that are necessary for it to operate. Like a motor car which, unless we feed it with petrol and oil, won't go, or if we feed it with poor-quality fuel and lubricants, functions ineffectively, so too will our body. A regular, balanced food intake is essential for a regular, balanced body. Set a pattern, adjust your body to it, and forget those crazy one-week diets which do nothing but reduce the credibility of those who write them.

Soups are a marvellous way of getting good food with plenty of flavour, and they are easy to cook.

LEMON SOUP
Serves 4

INGREDIENTS

5 cups good chicken stock
125 g (4 oz) rice
3 egg yolks
juice of 2 lemons

METHOD

- Bring the stock to the boil. Add the rice, and cook until it is tender (about 9 minutes).
- Beat the egg yolks with the lemon juice, then add a little of the hot stock. Pour this mixture into the soup, stirring constantly, and continue to cook for another 10 minutes.
- Serve very hot.

GAZPACHO
Serves 6

INGREDIENTS

tomato soup (see page 95)
1 green capsicum, chopped
½ teaspoon Indian curry powder
salt
freshly ground black pepper
ice cubes
½ raw onion, finely grated
1 egg per person
cultured sour cream
parsley

METHOD

- Start with tomato soup and add some chopped green capsicum, Indian curry powder, salt, freshly ground black pepper, lots of ice cubes, and some finely grated raw onion.
- While the ice is chilling the soup, prepare the eggs. Separate the eggs, and lightly poach the yolks. (You can keep the egg whites to make a pavlova or a whisky sour.)
- Slip the poached yolk into a soup bowl and then carefully pour the soup and ice over it.
- To serve, add a whirl of sour cream and a sprig of parsley.

Hot encounter

'The Indians are coming! The Indians are coming!' screamed from the screens of the Saturday arvo flicks in most city and country cinemas throughout Australia when I was a boy.

Roy Rogers, Tom Mix, Hopalong Cassidy, and Buffalo Bill were among the best of the good guys who out-gunned and out-glamoured the pesky Indians who, feather bedecked, rode bareback through the canyons and swept out on to the prairies. Flapping their hands in front of their mouths they threatened havoc until either the Cavalry or individual good guys gave them a thorough pasting.

But the cry 'Here come the Indians! Here come the Indians!' also echoed around the hills outside Tumut, where I grew up.

The Indians in question were from the subcontinent of India and travelled in a covered wagon not dissimilar to that which the American Red Indians attacked during the Saturday afternoon matinees. This Indian family sold herbs and spices, bolts of cloth and bottled sauces, along with curry powders and beads and trinkets. The family consisted of husband and wife, and a tribe of brown-skinned kids with flashing dark eyes and dazzlingly white teeth. Unlike the occasional gypsy caravan that clattered through the hills, the Indians didn't nick anything that wasn't tied down.

Often they would camp in a paddock or beside the road, and cook their curries in camp ovens which emitted the fragrant and exotic smells of their homeland.

They carried out unofficial cooking classes for the locals who either walked or rode their horses to sit around the campfire and be taught the mysteries of the Punjab, Calcutta, Bengal and other romantic names that we'd read in copies of *Boys' Own* and *Champion* comic books or hard-bound copies of *The Life of a Bengal Lancer*.

I must remind you, dear reader, that to convince an Aussie bushie to eat garlic or chilli was an achievement. As you know, roast leg of mutton, peas and potatoes was pretty much standard fare. A mixed grill was considered exotic and so curries were not called for often and, if they were, they were treated cautiously.

But somehow the Indians cast a magic spell, and those who visited the campsite consumed the curries with much merriment and jugs of ice-cold water dipped from the mountain streams.

Any number of rabbits could be chased from their burrows by ferrets or small dogs. The rabbits would be expertly gutted and skinned, chopped into pieces, and cooked with the simmering onions and spices.

The Aussies cooked great pots full of mashed potatoes on which to serve and de-flame the curry. Some of the older returned soldiers from the World War I skited they'd eaten a lot hotter from the kitchens of the Gippos and Sheikhs of the Desert.

I remember warmly (or in the case of the food, with a deal of heat) the visits of the Indians. They were a happy, courteous family who enriched our lives and our cooking pots.

Sauces
SIMPLE
AND LONGER

A sauce is a sauce, of course, of course

It shouldn't be, but it is often, a source of annoyance to me to have prepared and served food with a sauce which has been diligently designed to complement all other aspects of the meal, and then to have someone ask, 'Got any salt and pepper, mate?' It sends shudders through my soul.

The patient reply of, 'It's in the sauce, my friend' is usually answered with a, 'Yeah, but I always put salt and pepper on m'food.'

Or, 'Do you have any chilli? Or chutney? Tomato sauce, Worcestershire or soy?'

It's hard not to headbutt the nearest double-boiler and scream, 'I've made the bloody sauce to suit the occasion and I don't want you or anyone else mucking about with the balance which has been assayed as gold at the Mines Department.'

Strewth, gentle reader, I'm sure you can understand my position. Sure, if someone is sitting in my restaurant and orders, say, a fish but doesn't want the sauce I've prepared, I will happily produce another. Or if they wish more salt or even cayenne pepper, they're paying for the meal so it's their prerogative. But not if they're guests at my dinner table.

Even with wine, some people must think one is a hotel and therefore stock all of the most exotic of the exotics. For instance, you don't sit your guests down and say, 'Would you like roast beef, snapper, crown of lamb or Irish Stew?' They are there to share your fare with you.

With this attitude you can see I have no compunction in saying, 'I'm sorry if what's put in front of you is considered inedible, I'm sure you can fill in your time with conversation until the next course arrives. If not, maybe you would like to dial a pizza.' That applies, in my opinion, whether people are being fed in your dining room, on your patio or standing around a barbecue in the backyard or by a babbling brook.

But you may not be as ornery as me, and therefore need to produce a selection of sauces for your next outdoor happening.

QUICK, EASY, FOOLPROOF, FUN WAYS TO MAKE SAUCES IN SECONDS

- Mix into commercial tomato sauce: the juice of a lemon, a little sour cream, and chopped red and green capsicum, along with some finely diced onion. And, as a further option, you may wish to finely dice garlic — peel the skin and soften the cloves in boiling water first.

- Try soy sauce, sweetened with honey, garlic juice, cracked black pepper, and definitely no salt. Also soy sauce mixed with a fair quantity of sour cream makes a marvellous sauce.

- Hoy Sin sauce, straight out of the bottle, or wet with the juice of a lemon makes a fabulous sauce, as does commercial plum sauce with a little lemon juice and sour cream.

- In fact, any of the commercial sauces may be added to with a little imagination.

- I believe it's a good plan not to put the sauce over the food you serve but to the side of it. This allows your guests to take as much or as little of the sauce as they wish to satisfy their palate.

- And, by the way, the sauce can be as thick or as thin as you wish. There are really no rules any more unless you go back to the days of Escoffier and there you'll find iron-bound attitudes. No, today, if you want a strawberry sauce, throw the strawberries in a blender with the juice of a lemon, garlic salt, a pinch of garam masala, and some cracked pepper. Blend it, and you have your sauce.

- Carrots or cauliflower are much the same. They can even be combined. Soften carrots and cauliflower in boiling water, throw them into the blender with a goodly amount of sour cream, some garlic salt, cumin and coriander, and blend them.

- In fact, the blender has made the sauce-makers' work as easy as pie, but that's another book.

Gingered Gravy

Ingredients

1 tablespoon olive oil
1 small white onion, finely chopped
1 clove garlic, crushed
½ stick celery, sliced
½ small carrot, grated
60 g (2 oz) mushrooms, sliced
pinch dried thyme leaves
freshly ground black pepper
2 teaspoons tomato paste
2 cups beef stock
1 teaspoon soy sauce
¼ teaspoon finely chopped fresh root ginger

Method

- Heat the oil in a heavy-based saucepan, toss in the onion, garlic, celery, carrot and mushrooms. Sprinkle with the thyme and freshly ground black pepper, and sauté until the vegetables are soft.

- Stir in the tomato paste. Pour in the stock, add the soy sauce and ginger, stir and bring to the boil. Let it boil, uncovered, until it reduces and thickens.

- Serve dribbled over slices of cooked meat.

SALAD DRESSING WITH RASPBERRY VINEGAR

INGREDIENTS

olive oil
raspberry vinegar (see below)
lemon juice
1 clove garlic, crushed
freshly ground black pepper

METHOD

- Put some olive oil into a long, narrow glass container which has a tight-fitting lid. Next add raspberry vinegar, almost the same quantity as the oil. Make the vinegar quantity the same as the oil by adding lemon juice.

- Add the garlic and some freshly ground black pepper. Put on the lid, and shake until all the ingredients are well mixed.

RASPBERRY VINEGAR

METHOD

- Put a handful of raspberries — don't crush them — into a bottle with a slice of lemon peel. Fill the bottle with white vinegar and leave for 2 weeks before using.

MUSTARD SAUCE

INGREDIENTS

4 tablespoons French mustard
1 teaspoon dry mustard
2 tablespoons caster sugar
2 tablespoons white vinegar
½ cup vegetable oil
¼ cup chopped fresh dill

METHOD

- Make a paste of the two mustards, sugar and vinegar, then slowly whisk in the oil until it is thick and smooth. Stir in the dill, and keep in an airtight jar in the fridge until you need it. Give it a shake to combine all the ingredients before using it.

- Excellent served with slices of smoked salmon and thin slices of toast.

HORSERADISH AND CREAM SAUCE

INGREDIENTS

1 tablespoon prepared horseradish
1 tablespoon Dijon mustard
½ cup thickened cream

METHOD

• Stir the horseradish and mustard into the cream until it is thoroughly combined.

• Very good served with smoked trout and thin sandwiches of brown bread and butter with the crusts cut off.

SCALLOP SAUCE

INGREDIENTS

12 scallops
1 cup chicken stock

METHOD

• Warm the scallops under hot running water, then pop them into a blender with the chicken stock. Blend until very smooth. Add more chicken stock if you want a thinner consistency.

• Pour the sauce into a small saucepan, warm through gently (DON'T let it boil); then pour it over grilled redfin or any other grilled fish.

MAYONNAISE

INGREDIENTS

2 egg yolks
1 tablespoon white vinegar* or lemon juice
pinch of salt
pinch of dry mustard
freshly ground black pepper
1 ¼ cups olive oil

* *if you prefer, substitute tarragon vinegar for white vinegar*

METHOD

- Whisk together the egg yolks, vinegar or lemon juice, salt, pepper and mustard, then whisk in the oil, pouring it in very, very slowly at first. You can gradually pour it in more quickly, but you must make sure that you keep whisking all the time.

- If you have a blender, put the egg yolks into the blender with the salt, then switch the blender on to a low setting and slowly pour in the vinegar or lemon juice, then the olive oil, mustard and pepper. If by any chance the mayonnaise curdles, don't worry; just pour out the curdled mayonnaise (but don't throw it away). Wash and dry the blender, put another egg yolk into the blender, setting at a low speed, and slowly pour in the curdled mayonnaise.

TIPS

- If the mayonnaise is thin or has curdled:

The egg yolks and oil weren't the same temperature when you mixed them.

The egg yolks and oil weren't at room temperature when you used them.

You didn't add the vinegar or lemon juice to the egg yolks before the oil. (The acid helps prevent curdling.)

- If it has a bad flavour, the oil was stale or had been used for cooking.

- If it has a harsh taste, you probably used malt vinegar.

GREEN TOMATO CHUTNEY

INGREDIENTS

2.5 kg (5 lb) green tomatoes, sliced
500 g (1 lb) onions, chopped
1 tablespoon peppercorns
1 tablespoon salt
sprinkle of dried basil leaves
2 cups sugar
4 cups vinegar
1½ cups raisins
1½ cups sultanas
1 clove garlic, crushed

METHOD

- Place the tomatoes and onions in a deep basin with the peppercorns, salt and basil.
- Leave them until the next day. Boil the sugar in the vinegar, add the raisins and sultanas, and simmer for 5 minutes.
- Add the garlic, the tomatoes and onion mixture, and simmer gently until the chutney thickens.

HUNGARIAN PAPRIKA SAUCE

INGREDIENTS

2 tablespoons olive oil
1 small onion, finely chopped
1 tablespoon paprika
1 cup chicken stock
½ cup dry white wine
salt
¼ cup thickened cream

METHOD

- Heat the oil in a saucepan, and gently sauté the onion until it is transparent.
- Stir in the paprika, then the stock and white wine. Bring to the boil, and continue to boil until the sauce has reduced and started to thicken. Add a little salt and the cream.
- Make sure the sauce is heated through, and serve with hot or cold chicken.

TOMATO SAUCE WITH ANCHOVIES

INGREDIENTS

2 tablespoons olive oil
4 cloves garlic, juiced
8 ripe tomatoes, chopped
8 anchovy fillets, chopped
2 level teaspoons mint, finely chopped
salt
freshly ground black pepper

METHOD

- Heat the oil in a saucepan, and drop in the juice of the garlic. Add the tomatoes, anchovies and mint. Sauté for 15 minutes, then season with salt and pepper.

- Allow the sauce to cool a little, then put it through the blender. Return it to the pan to continue simmering until it is thick.

Cold Meats
FOR A
HOT DAY

High hopes

As a young man, most of my mates seemed to do splendidly well with womenfolk. They always had someone to take to picnics or barbecues in their parents' backyards. But I was somewhat shy, unable to bring myself to attempt the boldness of my mates who, as cavalier and nonchalant as you please, would ask, 'I suppose a kiss is out of the question?' of the young ladies they ran into here, there and everywhere.

'It's easy, Peter,' snapped m'mate, Whacker Williams. 'They'll either say "Yes" or "No," and if it's "No" you try the next one. We're having a picnic down by the waterhole on Saturday and there'll be lots of lovely ladies looking for a likely lad like you, so bring along a leg of cold meat and a salad, and you'll be home and hosed.'

On the Friday I cooked up a shoulder of pork which I'd seasoned to a treat. On Saturday I arrived at the town's young people's favourite swimming hole which was a placid pool in the river surrounded by weeping willows.

A giggling, gay crowd of young men and women romped in and out of the water between making salads and sandwiches.

A gorgeous, leggy young blonde was buttering bread and it was her I sidled up to. 'Maybe you'd like a slice of my pork,' I purred bravely, handing the meat to her. 'And I suppose a kiss is out of the question?' I hurried on, following Whacker's instructions by sliding my arm around her slim waist.

Stars exploded behind my eyes as the pork came back to me with more force than it had been presented with.

I picked myself up to see her flounce off with, whom I later learned, her boyfriend.

Whacker found me sitting, dejected, on a log, a little later.

'How did you go, mate? Don't tell me you were given the cold shoulder again?'

'Yes I was, mate. Over the left ear.'

STUFFED LEG OF LAMB
Serves 6–8

INGREDIENTS

1 cup cooked brown rice
¼ cup dried fruit medley
(chopped dried apples, pears, apricots, peaches, etc)
good pinch of dried marjoram leaves
3 tablespoons plain yoghurt
1 clove garlic, crushed
1 x 1.5 kg (3 lb) leg of lamb, boned
¼ cup soft multi-grain breadcrumbs
¼ cup finely chopped onion
1 tablespoon honey

METHOD

- Mix together the rice, the fruit, and the marjoram. Stir in the yoghurt. Add a bit of garlic, then stuff the leg of lamb with the mixture. Put the lamb into the oven to cook at 190°C (375°F) for 50 minutes per kilogram.

- Just about 10 minutes before the meat is cooked, slip it out of the oven, mix together the breadcrumbs, onion, a little more garlic and marjoram and stir in some honey. Spread that on the outside of the lamb and pop it back in the oven to finish cooking. The honey melts in and browns, and the breadcrumbs, onion and garlic give a crusty finish.

GLAZED HAM

Serves 10–12

INGREDIENTS

1 ham
1½ cups brown sugar
2 teaspoons dry mustard
⅓ cup dried breadcrumbs
¼ cup orange juice
whole cloves
unpeeled apple rings

METHOD

• Heat the oven to 160°C (325°F), then put the ham on a rack, uncovered, in a shallow pan and cook, allowing about 1 hour per kilogram (2 lb). Take the ham out of the oven 30 minutes before it is cooked and while you are preparing the glaze, turn the oven temperature up to 200°C (400°F).

• Cut off the rind and all the fat, and cut shallow diagonal gashes in diamond shapes along the top side of the ham.

• Make a mixture of the brown sugar, mustard and breadcrumbs and cover the gashed side of the ham with it. Moisten it with the orange juice, and stud it with whole cloves and apple rings. Turn the oven down to 160°C (325°F) again and immediately put in the ham. Leave it there for 30 minutes, take it out of the oven, and allow to cool. Carve down towards the bone.

CORNED BEEF
Serves 10–12

INGREDIENTS

1 x 2 kg (4 lb) piece of silverside
1 cup water
1 teaspoon dried oregano leaves
freshly ground black pepper
1 carrot, peeled and sliced
1 white onion, stuck with 3 whole cloves
¼ cup chopped celery leaves
1 bay leaf

METHOD

* Put the silverside in a pressure cooker. Add enough water to cover the meat, and bring it to the boil without the lid on. Immediately drain off the water because that gets rid of all the excess salt. Now put the meat back into the pressure cooker, add 1 cup of fresh water, the oregano, freshly ground black pepper (NO SALT), carrot, onion, celery tops and bay leaf. Put the lid on, pop on the weight and place the cooker over a high heat. When the weight begins to jiggle, turn the heat down to low and cook for about 45 minutes.

* If you don't have a pressure cooker, just boil up the meat in a saucepan, then get rid of the salty water. Put the meat back into the saucepan with all the other ingredients. Cover with water, pop on a lid and bring to the boil. Lower the heat and simmer for 30 minutes. Then take the pan from the stove and wrap the whole lot up in a blanket — saucepan, lid and all — and leave overnight. By morning it will be cooked.

The fencing master

Alexandre Dumas was a great character. He wrote *The Count of Monte Cristo* and all that stuff — you know, *The Three Musketeers* — but he also wrote a cookbook which has become world famous.

So you see, he often put down the rapier and took up the knife and fork, although he sometimes didn't make the transition and used a giant toothpick to *touché* a tournedos or two.

He insisted that his sword was mightier than his pen. Not only did it carve up enemies, but it carved up entrées as well.

I don't know how true it is, but at a fencing practice Dumas swore he could cut up a selection of vegetables. What he did was lay out the carrots next to the parsnip, celery, sweet potato, rhubarb for desserts, and breadstick for starters. When they were in line, his sword flicked across their length, slicing all the food.

Every Wednesday evening at eleven o'clock (usually after the theatre and a few beakers of absinthe) his mates would drop in and they'd each make a course for a late night supper.

One artist who was very popular at the time always made an enormous omelette which he'd decorate with cleverly cut black and green olives, carrots and capsicum. He'd make the omelette, topped like a pizza, into an attractive picture. Celery tops and parsley were trees and bushes; he'd use food colouring in cream or cheese or the like to paint the sky and chopped parsley for the grass, and so on.

Anyway, every Wednesday night the result was terrific and every Wednesday the result was the same. Dumas advanced on the masterpiece with his sword drawn to cut the egg-cake. The artist would plead for time to admire his artistry, but the others, who were starving by that time, demanded it be eaten there and then.

A bit of buffeting went on as Dumas tried to sword the food. A fight erupted, other swords appeared and it'd be on! As the fight developed, so did the tempers, until some silly fellow tripped over the omelette, and they'd all end up rolling in it, with swords sawing omelette, arms or anything else.

Of course, the omelette was an awful disaster, but apart from the artists, who always ended up screaming about their lack of artistic integrity or understanding, the rest of the bandaged team knocked back a bottle or two (each!), started cooking, and carving hunks of meat from an ox Dumas would have constantly turning on a spit over his fire.

The ox liver sautéed while the kidneys bubbled in burgundy or whatever sauce they'd invented that evening.

But it's the carving I want to talk about. You should always cut across the grain. That way ensures you chew with the grain.

Most people reverse that, which simply means the sharp steel knife blade is cutting the easy way — with the grain — which makes you chew against it. That, of course, is wrong.

Good carving saves food and adds to the enjoyment of it. Bad carving wastes food, time and flavour. The essence of good carving is to allow the knife to do the cutting. The hand that holds the knife must guide it, not drive it.

How to carve your dinner

1 Stand up to carve.

2 Remove the fat.

3 Cut across the grain. Exception is with super-tender meat.

4 Cut down towards the bone.

5 With pork, cut between the crackling scores before carving. I always remove the crackling to cut it into neat pieces before I carve the pork.

6 Beef should be carved thinly; lamb and pork in 6 mm ($\frac{1}{4}''$) thick slices.

Sweet Thought
FOR A
SWEET TOOTH

Toffee Tom

I can only vaguely remember Tom who lived in the double-storey house, with a shopfront, next to the overgrown paddock on which an old grey mare grazed.

Tom was a stocky young bloke of about seven years old. He had a square face and freckles, tight curly nut-brown hair, round grandpa-type glasses, and a serious side which kept popping to the fore.

'I read a book the other night,' he started off the conversation, 'on how to make toffee. A cookbook for kids it was, with step-by-step pictures which even young nippers like us could follow easily.'

'Will your mum let you use the kitchen?' I asked incredulously.

'Of course not. But she's going out this arvo on a lamington drive for Red Cross.'

'Yeah, but she'll lock the kitchen,' I reasoned.

'Of course she will. But I've left the kitchen window latch unsnibbed, so if you pinch half a bag of sugar from your mum's kitchen, I'll do the same, and we'll make a saucepan or two full of toffee and they'll never know the difference after we've washed up.'

And so the great cooking adventure was set into operation. With more, much more thorough planning than Ronald Biggs and his

Great Train Robbers ever organised, two likely young lads set about carrying out their master plan.

I put a couple of cups of sugar in my schoolbag, flung it over my shoulder and set off down the road to Tom's place. On arriving, I bunked him through the window, and he hauled me in after him.

With no more ado, we set about sourcing the pans and producing the sugar.

I only had half of mine left as I discovered a hole in the bottom of my schoolbag. Nevertheless, progress we did.

'Get your book, Tom,' I cried, full of enthusiasm.

'Er ... yeah, well ... Mum's returned it, mate.'

'What?!' I snapped, pink cheeks flushing.

'It wasn't ours. She's given it back to the lady she borrowed it from,' answered Tom, crestfallen.

'Yeah? Well, now what?' I pleaded.

'Oh, don't worry,' Tom said suddenly breaking into a smile. 'I can remember the recipe. You put the sugar in a big saucepan, splash in some water and stick it over a high gas. The sugar dissolves, the water evaporates, and you end up with toffee.'

'Yeah?' I queried. 'And how does the white sugar go brown?'

'Er ... yeah, well. Do you reckon I've forgotten something?'

'Maybe we should use brown sugar to start with,' I suggested.

'We haven't got any brown sugar. Anyway,' Tom snapped, 'most things go brown when you cook 'em, so maybe the sugar does too.'

And so the pot was plonked on the gas, which was turned on flat out, the sugar and the water popped in and stirred before Tom and I climbed out the window to kick the footy about the backyard while our mixture turned to toffee.

It was the smoke pouring out the kitchen window which reminded us of our culinary duties.

We scrambled back through the window to find that, indeed, the white sugar had changed colour. It had gone beyond brown to black. It had also vulcanised itself to the aluminium saucepan which reacted violently to Tom pouring cold water in it. We lost each other in clouds of steam which mingled with the smoke.

We buried the blackened saucepan in the backyard with a solemn oath to never again attempt to make toffee.

My mother arrived soon after the burial, having followed the trail of sugar from her kitchen to Tom's mum's kitchen.

By then, thankfully, the smoke and steam had cleared, but the smell hadn't.

I mumbled three or four different versions of why I had taken the sugar and what had become of it. My mother believed none of them and took me home by the ear.

Tom and his mother moved out of town to live in the big smoke. I don't believe for a moment our kitchen capers had anything to do with the decision, but Tom was not allowed to play with me again and, indeed, I never saw him again.

I often wonder if archaeologists in the future may unearth our pot and ponder the reasons for its ritual burial and its asphalt-like filling.

AUSTRALIA'S OWN PAVLOVA
Serves 10–12

INGREDIENTS

6 egg whites
pinch of salt
1 ¼ cups caster sugar
1 teaspoon cornflour
1 teaspoon vinegar
1 teaspoon vanilla essence
2 cups whipped cream

METHOD

- Line the bottoms of two upturned 20 cm (8″) sandwich tins with greaseproof paper, and pin a band of greaseproof paper around the outside of the tins to support the pavlova as it rises.

- Put the egg whites in a warm, dry mixing bowl, add the pinch of salt and beat hard for about 2 minutes until the whites are stiff. (Only glass, glazed pottery or metal bowls should be used.) Constantly beating, add the sugar a little at a time; then continue beating and add the cornflour, vinegar and vanilla essence.

- Spoon the mixture into each of the tins, and pop them into the oven at 120°C (250°F) and cook for an hour. Take them out of the oven, let them cool until they're cold, then peel off the paper.

- Sandwich together with some whipped cream. You can flavour the cream with a dash of brandy or rum. Then decorate the top with strawberries, passionfruit or a mixture of fruit.

BANANAS WITH CITRUS AND CREAM
Serves 3

INGREDIENTS

2 tablespoons butter
1 tablespoon brown sugar
3 firm bananas
splash of cherry brandy and Grand Marnier
juice of an orange
juice of a lemon
freshly ground black pepper
$^2/_3$ cup cream

METHOD

- Melt the butter in a large heavy frying pan, throw in the brown sugar, and stir until it is melted.

- Peel the bananas and cut them in half lengthwise, then carefully place them in the butter sauce.

- Pour in a splash of cherry brandy, a splash of Grand Marnier, and the orange and lemon juice. Stir to blend, being careful not to break up the bananas.

- Sprinkle with freshly ground black pepper to cut down the sweetness, then slowly stir in the cream. Warm through — but don't cook — the bananas, then serve them with some sauce spooned over the top.

PASSIONFRUIT LOAF
Makes 12–15 slices

INGREDIENTS

⅓ cup butter
½ cup caster sugar
2 eggs
pulp of 3 passionfruit
milk
2 cups self-raising flour
pinch of salt

ICING

INGREDIENTS

1 cup icing sugar
½ teaspoon butter, softened
pulp of 1 passionfruit
milk

METHOD

- Cream the butter and sugar together until they are light and fluffy, then gradually beat in the eggs. Put the passionfruit pulp into a bowl, and add sufficient milk to give ⅔ cup of liquid. Fold the flour and salt into the butter, sugar and eggs mixture, and then gradually beat in the passionfruit and milk. Keep beating until the mixture is smooth and creamy.

- Butter a 20 cm x 10 cm (8" x 4") loaf tin. Pour the mixture into it, and bake at 180°C (350°F) for about an hour or until a skewer inserted in the top comes out clean. Take the loaf out of the oven, and allow to cool while you make the icing.

- Sift the icing sugar, stir in the softened butter, passionfruit pulp and enough milk to make a stiff paste. Pop the bowl over a dish of hot water and stir until the icing is spreadable; then quickly spread over the top of the cooled passionfruit loaf.

LIME CHIFFON PIE
Serves 10–12

INGREDIENTS

1 packet lime flavour jelly
½ cup boiling water
2 eggs
1 pre-baked shortcrust pastry case (18–20 cm/7–8″)
½ cup whipped cream
grated rind of 1 lemon for garnish

METHOD

- Put the jelly and water into a saucepan over a very low heat, stirring all the time, until the jelly dissolves. Take it off the heat and let it cool until it is just beginning to thicken and set.

- Separate the eggs, beat the egg yolks and gradually whisk in the cooled jelly. Whisk the egg whites until they are stiff, then gently fold in the jelly and egg-yolk mixture. Pile it into the pastry case and pop it in the fridge to chill.

- Before serving, decorate with whipped cream and sprinkle with grated lemon rind.

FROZEN EGGNOG
Serves 6

INGREDIENTS

5 eggs
1³/₄ cups sugar
pinch of mace
³/₄ cup brandy
2 cups cream

METHOD

- Separate the eggs and beat the yolks with the sugar until they're pale and creamy, then stir in the mace and brandy.

- Whisk the egg whites until they are stiff. Then in another bowl whip the cream until that is stiff too. Fold the egg whites into the yolk and brandy mixture, and then fold in the cream.

- Spoon it into ice-cream trays and pop them into your freezer. When it is set serve it like ice-cream.

CREAM CHEESE AND ALMOND TART
Serves 10–12

INGREDIENTS
155 g (5 oz) shortcrust pastry
3 eggs
1 ¼ cups cream cheese
1 tablespoon sugar
1 ½ tablespoons melted butter
1 tablespoon plain flour
⅓ cup cream
½ cup blanched almonds, chopped

METHOD

- Roll out your shortcrust pastry until it is about 3 mm (⅛") thick, then 'blind bake' it in a 23 cm (9") tart tin. To blind bake a pastry shell you line the tart tin with the pastry, and then put some greaseproof paper over the base of the pastry. Weigh the paper down with dried beans or rice so that when it is cooking the pastry doesn't bubble up. Cook it in a hot oven at 200°C (400°F) for about 20 minutes. When it's cooked, take the tin out of the oven and let the pastry cool with the beans still weighing it down. While the pastry case is cooling make your filling.

- Separate the eggs and put the egg yolks, cream cheese, sugar, melted butter, flour and cream into a big mixing bowl, and mix them all together well. Sprinkle in the chopped almonds and stir it around so that they are spread evenly through the mixture.

- Now beat the egg whites until they are nice and stiff, and fold them into the cheese mixture in the big bowl.

- Take the beans and paper out of the pastry case, pour the cheese mixture into it, and then pop it in the oven and cook it at 180°C (350°F) for about 25 to 30 minutes until the filling is set and is a nice golden-brown.

- You can eat the tart either hot or cold.

OUR CHOCOLATE MOUSSE
Serves 4

INGREDIENTS

100 g (3 oz) cooking chocolate
2 eggs, separated
1 cup cream
¼ cup caster sugar
dash of rum, brandy or liqueur

METHOD

- Melt the chocolate in a bowl over hot water. Stir in the egg yolks until smooth, then gradually blend in the cream.
- Whip the egg whites with the caster sugar to form a stiff meringue. Then fold this into the chocolate mixture.
- Fold in a dash of rum, brandy or liqueur, and pour the mixture into 4 individual dishes. Pop them into the fridge to chill for a few hours.
- Decorate with whipped cream and almonds or cherries.

My father's diet

At theology college my father was known as Porky Pete. He was a huge man both vertically and horizontally, but fortunately he lived during an age which accepted the portly figure as being a symbol of success.

My father's Kim Beazley proportions exuded warmth and well-being. His comfortable figure exuded confidence. The only people who frowned at my father were his doctors.

'You must shed some lard, old fella,' he was told. 'Your ticker can't possibly keep pumping blood through the thousands of miles of arteries and veins that are needed to keep your huge frame alive and kicking.'

I was mightily surprised when, one day, the old boy agreed to go on a diet. And even more surprised when he stuck to it — or so I thought.

At meal times he shunned sugar and cream. 'Get thee behind me, Satan!' he would thunder pointing, with a quivering figure, at the proffered sweets.

Some weeks later I was asked to take his suit to the drycleaners, so I dutifully picked up the huge amount of cloth and went through the pockets to make sure there was nothing of importance which may suffer at the cleaners.

I withdrew my hand from one pocket sticky with brown stuff. The pocket was choc-a-block full of coconut and chocolate rum balls. It would seem once he had fled the family dining table he would stoke massive quantities of these little fat-makers into his mouth.

My mother confronted him with his treachery, which he denied angrily. No one believed him of course and, anyway, next day he was back into the cream and caramel sauces, Turkish delights and an array of other tempting treats which kept him happily fat for the rest of his life.

BYRON BAY SALAD

Serves 4–6

INGREDIENTS

1 honeydew melon
225 g (7 oz) fresh lychees, peeled and stoned

DRESSING

INGREDIENTS

300 ml (10 fl oz) cream
3 tablespoons chopped preserved ginger
4 tablespoons Advocaat
grated rind of 1 lemon

METHOD

- Scoop out the flesh of the melon with a melon baller, and pile the balls together with the lychees into a serving bowl.
- Lightly whip the cream, stir in the ginger, Advocaat and lemon rind, and serve in a separate bowl alongside the melon and lychees.

GINGER AND LEMON WATER ICE
Serves 4–6

INGREDIENTS

225 g (7 oz) sugar
450 ml (15 fl oz) water
175 ml (5½ fl oz) lemon juice
75 g (2½ oz) preserved root ginger, very finely chopped

METHOD

- Dissolve the sugar in the water over a gentle heat, stirring often, then bring to the boil and boil for 5 minutes. Take the pan from the heat, and let the syrup cool. Stir in the lemon juice and ginger.

- Pour the mixture into a shallow freezer container and put it into the freezer, set at its coldest setting. Leave until it starts to freeze around the edge, then turn it out into a chilled bowl and beat it to get rid of the ice crystals. Put it back into the freezer until it is solid.

- Take it from the freezer 15 minutes before you want to serve it.

Cheese For
OUTDOORS

It ain't funny!

The cameras stood like giant insects on spindly legs. The lens, the one eye of Olympus, peering from its plastic shell. Sound men with boom mikes, which looked like headless grey Persian cats on long poles, worried over the boxes of spinning spools that were draped around their necks. The rest of the crew, bearded and leather jacketed, drank the ubiquitous coffee and ate the inevitable sticky bun.

I fidgeted beside the hammock from which I was to deliver my lines for the Australian Dairy Corporation's butter commercial.

The ad was designed to convey that we should be eating healthier, natural foods.

I was to nonchalantly swing in the hammock as I delivered the message straight down the throat of the camera. With an unhurried flick of the wrist I was to lob a corn cob on to the lit barbecue. But first, the husk of the corn was peeled back, the 'silk' removed, and the kernels spread with butter and sprinkled lightly with garlic salt and a little dried basil. The husks were then pulled back up, and secured with a twist of oven wire.

After a close-up shot of the corn, the camera was to come back to me as I completed the message and reiterated that the dairy

158

industry of Australia was an important one and we should all be proud of it.

Well, all went well up until the nonchalant flick of the wrist. Oh, the corn sailed through the air and accurately landed on the barbecue. Unfortunately, I also sailed through the air and landed on my bum.

The gaffer had set the hammock swinging gently, but my nonchalant flick of the wrist shifted my body weight, which then flung the hammock into an attempted figure eight. Of course, this uncontrollable piece of woven cloth had been set up next to the swimming pool. My posterior thudded on to the tiles at the water's edge. With a startled scream and much gyrating of arms and legs, I plopped into the pool and sank in a most undignified fashion.

It was some time before the crew undoubled itself from laughing and rescued their star in, what seemed to me, a most casual and unhurried manner.

My running make up would have put Marilyn Monroe's crying scene in *Big River* to shame.

After I was dried, dusted and divvyed over, we secured the wayward hammock to a nearby sapling, and I reluctantly scrambled back into the cocoon.

This time the flick of the wrist was very furtive and the smile somewhat uncertain, but the ad was successful because the Dairy Corporation and their editors, in their wisdom, ran the first take which showed the full splendour of my ducking.

We humans loved Charlie Chaplin best when he slipped on a banana skin, or Laurel and Hardy when they copped a pie in the face. We laughted hardest when the Keystone cops fell out of their erratically driven police car, and so the TV audience laughed at my dilemma.

Whether they bought more dairy product or not it was not revealed to me, but I was asked to write a series of ads where I would make Bud Abbott and Lou Costello look like sensible and sane citizens.

And here are some of the recipes which I designed using dairy food for a barbecue picnic.

PIQUANT CHEESE SLICE
Serves 10–12

INGREDIENTS

375 g (12 oz) shortcrust pastry
1 cup tasty cheese, grated
2¼ cups rolled oats
1 tablespoon water
1 dessertspoon prepared mustard
freshly ground black pepper
salt
pinch of dried basil leaves
1½ tablespoons butter, melted

METHOD

- Divide the pastry in two, and roll out one lot thinly, to about 3 mm (⅛") thick. Line a well-buttered 28 cm x 18 cm (11" x 7") shallow baking tin with the pastry. Now mix together the cheese, oats, water, mustard, freshly ground black pepper, salt and basil, then stir in the melted butter.

- Spread the cheese mixture over the pastry. Roll the rest of the pastry out to 3 mm (⅛") thick, and place it on top of the mixture. Pinch the edges of the pastry together to seal in the cheese, then bake in the oven at 190°C (375°F) for about half an hour. You can eat the slice hot or cold.

POTTED PORT CHEESE
Serves 10

INGREDIENTS

1 cup grated tasty cheese
³/₄ cup grated Mozzarella cheese
½ teaspoon French mustard
salt
freshly ground black pepper
½ teaspoon Worcestershire sauce
dash of Tabasco sauce
3 tablespoons port

METHOD

- Mix all the ingredients together thoroughly, then put the mixture into a small bowl, cover, and pop it in the fridge for 24 hours.
- Serve with crunchy bread or crackers.

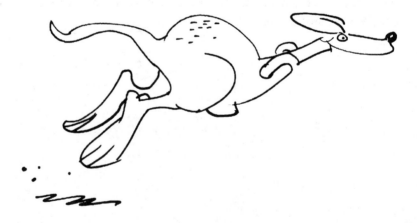

CHEESE PAKORAS
Serves 4–6

INGREDIENTS

2 cups flour
½ teaspoon ground coriander
½ teaspoon turmeric
½ teaspoon cayenne
1 clove garlic, crushed
pinch baking soda
1½ cups water
juice of 1 lemon
250 g (8 oz) processed cheddar cheese, cubed
2 cups olive oil

METHOD

- Combine the flour, coriander, turmeric, cayenne, garlic and baking soda. Add the water gradually, stirring all the time until you have a thick, smooth batter, then stir in the lemon juice. Put the cheese cubes into the batter, and stir them around until they are thoroughly coated and no cheese can be seen.

- Heat the oil in a saucepan, and when it is hot carefully drop the coated cheese cubes in and cook until they are golden-brown. Lift them out with a slotted spoon, pop them on to paper towel to drain, then serve.

BLUE BRIE TARTS
Makes 18

INGREDIENTS

250 g (8 oz) shortcrust pastry
350 g (11 oz) blue brie, rind removed
3 tablespoons cream
3 eggs, lightly beaten

METHOD

- Roll out the pastry to 3 mm (⅛") thickness. Cut out 18 circles and line 18 small tart tins. Prick the bases with a fork, cover with greaseproof paper, and fill with dried beans or rice. Bake in the oven at 220°C (450°F) for 10 minutes. Take them from the oven, leave for 2 minutes, then remove the paper and beans or rice.

- Chop the brie into small pieces, place in the top of a double-boiler or in a bowl set over a pan of simmering water, and add the cream. Stir for 4 minutes or until the cheese melts. Take it from the heat, and let the cheese mix cool slightly. Stir in the beaten egg.

- Pour about 1½ teaspoonsful of the mixture into each tart case. Bake at 180°C (350°F) for about 15 minutes or until puffed and golden.

LIPTAUER CHEESE
Serves 6–8

INGREDIENTS

450 g (14½ oz) cottage cheese
½ teaspoon sweet paprika
1 teaspoon caraway seeds
1 teaspoon mustard powder
1 teaspoon capers
1 teaspoon finely chopped chives or spring onions
2 tablespoons plain yoghurt
1 tablespoon beer, preferably Pilsener
radishes and onion to garnish

METHOD

- Push the cottage cheese through a sieve with a wooden spoon into a large bowl.
- Mix in enough paprika to colour the cheese a faint pink. Stir in the caraway seeds, mustard, capers and chives or spring onions.
- Add the yoghurt and beer, and mix all the ingredients together until thoroughly blended.
- Put the cheese in a mound on a dish, and surround it with radishes, slices of raw onion and slices of wholemeal or rye bread. This cheese will keep in the fridge for several days.

What You Knead To
KNOW ABOUT
BREAD AND BISCUITS

Mr Butcher, the baker, makes an Aussie icon

The First Fleet left Botany Bay in disarray. Taut sails dragged the bucking hulks with their cargoes of desolate convicts through the petulant waters which heap between North and South Head. Botany Bay was no place for a settlement — fresh water was virtually non-existent, the tangled scrub grew to the waterline and there was no safe anchorage.

Captain Phillip, RN, soon to be Governor Phillip, realised Port Jackson just around the corner was a far better bet. But he must hasten to beat the French in securing a foothold as well as unfurling his Union Jack from the nearest gum tree.

In their haste, and with the mercurial winds thwarting them, the British, after an embarrassing display of seamanship, the odd ramming and bottom scrape, made exit and entered Port Jackson, soon to become Sydney Harbour, named after Lord Sydney of the Old Country.

On the way out, the Fleet had stocked up with a menagerie of live animals from South Africa, and these and the convicts were off-loaded with Mr Butcher, the baker, who made a fire in the sand and, with flour and water, cooked Australia's first damper. Now about the only people who cook damper are boy scouts and, I assume, girl scouts as they now 'dib dib dob dob' happily together.

Mr Butcher's recipe was flour and water kneaded into dough which was then held over the hot coals to brown and cook out the flour flavour.

The First Fleet had no butter or blackberry jam but, if you do, spread your flour and water damper liberally for, dear cook, it needs it!

DROVER'S DAMPER

INGREDIENTS

3 cups self-raising flour
½ cup full-cream powdered milk
½ teaspoon salt
3 tablespoons butter
1 ½ cups water

METHOD

- Mix (preferably sift) the flour and the powdered milk together with the salt, at least two or three times. Rub the butter into the mix with your fingertips, and then work it into a soft dough with the water.

- Stir the mixture well with a broad-bladed knife, and place the mixture on a well-floured surface. Knead lightly until the dough can be picked up.

- Place the dough in a deep baking dish that has been greased, brush over with milk, and bake in a very hot camp oven for 20 minutes. Reduce the flames or coals about the oven and bake for a further 10 minutes or until the top of the damper sounds hollow when tapped.

- If using greased aluminium foil in place of a baking dish, allow ample room for expansion when wrapping the dough.

POTATO BREAD

2 cups self-raising flour
½ teaspoon salt
1 teaspoon sugar
¾ cup mashed potatoes
1 ¼ cups milk
¼ teaspoon nutmeg

METHOD

- Mix the flour and salt together well, and sift if possible. Add the sugar and mashed potatoes, and rub in until the mixture looks like breadcrumbs.

- Make a well in the centre of the mixture, add the milk and nutmeg, and mix into a dough. Knead on a floured surface until smooth.

- Form into a loaf, and place in a small but deep greased baking dish. Brush with milk and bake in a moderate camp oven for about 40 minutes or until the surface is golden-brown.

- If using greased aluminium foil instead of a baking dish, allow ample room for expansion when wrapping the dough.

JOHNNY CAKES
Makes 12–15

INGREDIENTS

1.5 kg (3 lb) plain flour
1 teaspoon salt
3 teaspoons cream of tartar
15 g (½ oz) bicarbonate soda
water

METHOD

- Mix all the ingredients together with a little water until you have a light dough. Knead for 5 minutes. Shape small dampers about as big as the palm of your hand, and pat out very thinly.

- Dredge with flour to prevent sticking. Spread the fire well out and put the Johnny Cakes on top of the hot coals; after 2 minutes turn them over.

- When cooked, split them open as you would a scone. They're good with butter and a slice of steak, or plenty of wild honey — they will satisfy the most ravenous appetites.

ZUCCHINI LOAF
Makes 12–15 slices

INGREDIENTS

1 onion, thinly sliced
4 zucchinis, thinly sliced lengthways (use a vegetable peeler)
4 eggs
¼ cup flour
250 g (8 oz) smooth ricotta cheese
½ cup grated Romano cheese
1 teaspoon dried oregano
freshly ground black pepper
1 tomato, thinly sliced
2 extra tablespoons grated Romano cheese

METHOD

- Heat a little oil in a frying pan, and gently cook the onion and zucchini for 5 minutes.

- In a bowl, mix together the eggs, flour, ricotta and Romano cheeses, and oregano. Add the onion and zucchini, and freshly ground black pepper.

- Pour the mixture into a 20 cm x 10 cm (8″ x 4″) greased and lined loaf pan. Decorate with tomato slices and extra Romano cheese.

- Bake at 180°C (350°F) for 50 minutes or until set and golden-brown.

RYE HERB LOAF

INGREDIENTS

125 g (4 oz) butter
1 large clove garlic, crushed
½ teaspoon salt
¼ teaspoon coarsely ground black pepper
¼ teaspoon crushed dried sage
¼ teaspoon chopped dried rosemary
¼ teaspoon dried thyme
¼ teaspoon dry mustard
¼ teaspoon dried tarragon
3 tablespoons finely chopped parsley
1 large loaf dark rye bread, sliced

METHOD

- Stir the butter to soften. Add the seasonings and mix well. Spread generously on slices of rye.

- Re-assemble loaf and wrap in foil. Heat at the side of the barbecue grill for 15–20 minutes until hot. Serve warm.

Apple Scone Wedges
Serves 4–8

Ingredients

2 cups plain flour
½ teaspoon salt
3 teaspoons baking powder
2 tablespoons butter
1 tablespoon caster sugar
1 medium-sized Granny Smith apple, peeled, cored and grated
½ cup milk
1 tablespoon dark brown sugar

Method

- Mix together the flour, salt and baking powder, then rub in the butter until it looks like fine breadcrumbs. Now stir in caster sugar and the apple. Slowly pour in the milk and mix until it is a soft dough.

- Turn out on to a lightly floured board and form into a round about 20 cm (8") across. Pop it on to an oiled baking sheet, brush the top of it with milk, and sprinkle with the brown sugar. Mark into 8 wedges, then bake in the oven at 200°C (400°F) for about 25 minutes or until golden-brown.

- Serve warm, broken into wedges, with butter.

GINGERBREAD PEOPLE
Makes 24

INGREDIENTS

1 cup treacle
1 teaspoon baking powder
¼ cup cold water
2 tablespoons rum
250 g (8 oz) butter
½ cup brown sugar
1 egg, beaten
4 cups plain flour
1 teaspoon salt
2 teaspoons ground ginger
½ teaspoon ground nutmeg
¼ teaspoon ground allspice
icing

METHOD

- Pour the treacle into a saucepan, then stir in the baking powder. When that is mixed in, add the water, rum, butter, sugar and beaten egg. Bring that slowly to the boil, then take off the heat and let it cool a little.

- Mix the flour, salt and spices together in a bowl, add the cooled liquid and make a dough. Cover the bowl and pop it in the fridge to chill overnight.

- Next day it should be ready to roll out; if it isn't, add a little more flour. Roll out the dough on a floured board until it's about 6 mm (¼″) thick, then cut our your gingerbread people, either with a gingerbread cutter if you have one, or by cutting round a paper pattern you have drawn and cut out.

- Use raisins for the eyes, then place the shapes on a buttered baking sheet and bake them for 12 minutes at 190°C (375°F). When they are cooked, take the tray out of the oven, and leave the gingerbread on it for a minute or two to cool a little. Pipe plain or coloured icing to make the mouth, hair and clothing.

INDEX

175